LEARNING FROM PRACTICE SERIES

Reflective Supervision

A learning and development manual

2nd Edition

Neil Thompson
and Peter Gilbert

Reflective Supervision

A learning and development manual, 2nd edition

Published by:
Pavilion Publishing and Media Ltd
Blue Sky Offices
Cecil Pashley Way
Shoreham by Sea
West Sussex
BN43 5FF

Tel: 01273 434 943
Email: info@pavpub.com

Published 2019

A catalogue record for this book is available from the British Library.

ISBN: 978-1-912755-46-2

Pavilion Publishing and Media is a leading publisher of books, training materials and digital content in mental health, social care and allied fields. Pavilion and its imprints offer must-have knowledge and innovative learning solutions underpinned by sound research and professional values.

Authors: Neil Thompson and Peter Gilbert
Production editor: Kristy Barker
Cover design: Phil Morash, Pavilion Publishing and Media Ltd.
Page layout and typesetting: Emma Dawe, Pavilion Publishing and Media Ltd.
Printing: Ashford Press

Contents

List of resources

All the resources needed to run the training exercises in this book can be downloaded at www.pavpub.com/learning-from-practice-resources/

Slides

Slide 1: Beginnings and endings

Slide 2: Giving feedback

Slide 3: The Kolb learning cycle

Slide 4: Mediation

Slide 5: Destructive processes in supervision

Slide 6: Balance of support and challenge

Slide 7: Good management vs bullying (1)

Slide 8: Good management vs bullying (2)

Slide 9: The four elements of supervision

Slide 10: Tools for promoting anti-discriminatory practice?

Worksheets

Worksheet 1: Preparing for supervision

Worksheet 2: Beginnings and endings

Worksheet 3: Giving feedback

Worksheet 4: Hopes and fears

Worksheet 5: Destructive processes in supervision

Worksheet 6: Quotes

Worksheet 7: Recording supervision

Worksheet 8: Managing poor performance

Worksheet 9: Promoting anti-discriminatory practice

Worksheet 10: Developing reflective practice

Worksheet 11: Avoiding the drama triangle

Handouts

Handout 1: Recording supervision

Handout 2: Avoiding the drama triangle

About the series

The *Learning from Practice* series offers a range of training and development resources for trainers, tutors and others involved in promoting learning. Each manual has been developed to serve as the basis for a training course or a staff development event and/or as part of a university or college module. Each of them assumes no specialist knowledge, either of the subject matter or of learning theory, although it is expected that users of the manual will have at least some familiarity with what is involved in running a training course or similar event.

Each manual contains useful background information about the subject matter covered so that the user of the resources can approach the subject matter with at least a basic knowledge of the key issues and, it is to be hoped, a desire to find out more from other available sources (which is why each manual has a *Guide to Further Learning* near the end, see p85). This background information is then followed by a series of exercises, each of which has step-by-step guidance for using the ideas in practice during an event.

There are also supplementary materials, although these will vary from manual to manual. Some include a PowerPoint file that can be used to form the basis of any presentations that need to be given as part of one or more exercises.

Of course, it is likely that experienced educators will want to consider adapting, extending or even combining elements from the exercises, and that can potentially work well. However, any such changes will need to be thought through very carefully and inexperienced trainers or tutors should perhaps run the exercises at least once as they stand before making any changes.

The series was originally published by Russell House Publishing, but this manual forms part of a set of new, revised and updated editions published by Pavilion Publishing as part of their range of high-quality learning and development resources.

The first editions of these resources were very well received, with considerable positive feedback. We trust you will find this new edition equally helpful, if not more so, and we wish you well in using the materials.

Other titles in the series

Developing Leadership by Peter Gilbert and Neil Thompson

Promoting Equality, Valuing Diversity by Neil Thompson

Responding to Loss by Bernard Moss and Neil Thompson

Spirituality, Meaning and Values by Bernard Moss and Neil Thompson

Tackling Bullying and Harassment in the Workplace by Neil Thompson

Working with Adults: Values into practice by Sue Thompson and Jackie Robinson

About this manual

Supervision is a process which, at best, can empower employees to fulfil their potential and to achieve optimal outcomes, making it a positive thing for all concerned: the individual employee; the supervisor, and the management team generally; the organisation as a whole; and the organisation's clients/service users/customers/patients. At its worst, it can be an oppressive, unproductive process of 'cat and mouse' in which the supervisor simply tries to 'check up' on the supervisee to make sure they are doing their job properly, while the latter does everything they can to avoid the former's attentions. This manual has been written to help ensure that supervision comes much closer to the former ideal than to the latter ordeal – for it to be genuinely *reflective* supervision.

Many supervisors are fortunate in that they have received high-quality supervision and are therefore well placed to put into practice what they have learned from such a positive experience. Others will have had a less positive experience of supervision, but there is still much learning to be gained from that, from looking at what has not been so helpful about the supervision received in order to make sure that the mistakes made are not repeated by a new generation of supervisors. Yet others may have had no experience of receiving supervision and now find themselves in a position of being expected to give it without necessarily understanding what it involves or how it is supposed to work. This manual should offer a platform for learning for all these supervisors, building on experiences of what works well and should therefore be used to the full, and what does not work at all and should therefore be avoided.

So, if you are in the business of helping supervisors develop their knowledge, skills and confidence, this manual should have a great deal of appeal for you.

Dr Neil Thompson
Series editor

The series editor

Dr Neil Thompson is an independent writer, educator and adviser. He has previously held full or honorary professorships at four UK universities and is now a sought-after trainer, consultant and conference speaker.

He has qualifications in social work, training and development, mediation and alternative dispute resolution and management (MBA), as well as a first-class honours degree, a doctorate (PhD) and a higher doctorate (DLitt). In 2011 he was presented with a Lifetime Achievement Award by BASW Cymru and in 2014 he was presented with the Dr Robert Fulton Award for excellence in the field of death, dying and bereavement by the Center for Death Education and Bioethics at the University of Wisconsin-La Crosse. He is a Fellow of the Chartered Institute of Personnel and Development and the Higher Education Academy and a Life Fellow of the Royal Society of Arts and the Institute of Welsh Affairs. In addition, he is a member of the International Work Group on Death, Dying and Bereavement.

Neil is a highly respected author, with more than 300 publications to his name, including several bestselling books. His recent publications include *The Social Worker's Practice Manual* (Avenue Media Solutions, 2018), *Mental Health and Well-being: Alternatives to the Medical Model* (Routledge, 2019) and *The Learning from Practice Manual* (Avenue Media Solutions, 2019).

He has been a speaker at conferences and seminars in the UK, Ireland, Italy, Spain, Norway, the Netherlands, Greece, the Czech Republic, Turkey, India, Hong Kong, Canada, the United States and Australia.

In his current role Neil offers:

▶ training, consultancy, mediation and expert witness services

▶ e-learning courses

▶ the Avenue Professional Development Programme, a subscription-based online learning community based on principles of self-directed learning and geared towards developing critically reflective practice

▶ online survey services to help organisations gauge how well they are doing in their people management efforts

▶ coaching and mentoring.

Information about his work, services and resources is available at www.NeilThompson. info. He has a YouTube channel at https://bit.ly/2O0E6OR and a free subscription to his *humansolutions* e-newsletter can be obtained at www.humansolutions.org.uk.

The authors

Dr Neil Thompson is an independent writer, educator and adviser. For further information about him, see the Series Editor section on the previous page.

Sadly, since the publication of the first edition of this manual, Peter Gilbert has passed away. Peter had a highly successful career, initially in the army, followed by 27 years' service in local government social services as a practitioner/manager and senior manager, rising to the level of Operations Director for Staffordshire County Council and then Director of Social Services for Worcestershire.

Following this, he became Professor of Social Work and Spirituality at Staffordshire University, where he was involved in giving spirituality a higher profile in relation to mental health and social care more broadly. In the latter years of his career he worked as an independent consultant in social and health care, while also serving as visiting professor at the University of Worcester.

Peter held a Master's in Modern History from Balliol College, Oxford; a Master's in Social Work from the University of Sussex; and an MBA from Roffey Park Management Institute/University of Sussex. His books include *Leadership: Being Effective and Remaining Human* (Russell House, 2007) and *Social Work and Mental Health: The Value of Everything* (2nd edn, Russell House, 2010).

Following his death, a book honouring his contributions was published by Pavilion: *Crossing the River: The contribution of spirituality to humanity and its future.*

Neil Thompson and Peter Gilbert are also the authors of a companion volume in the *Learning from Practice series* called *Developing Leadership.*

Preface

Getting the best out of staff owes so much to the skill and commitment of the supervisor. An effective supervisor is able to create win–win situations where everybody is happy: the employee fulfils their potential; the employers get the best return on their investment; and people who use the organisation's services benefit from the quality of the staff member's practice.

This important manual in the *Learning from Practice* series shows that supervision is not simply a matter of making sure that the supervisee is doing their job properly. It also involves helping staff achieve the best quality of work that they are capable of by maximising learning, promoting high levels of well-being and addressing any conflicts, tensions or other obstacles to optimal practice.

The manual provides background information about the role and significance of supervision and a set of learning exercises carefully designed to promote professional development. Anyone interested in promoting learning about supervision skills will find much of interest and use in this clear and well-written set of resources. Effective supervision is an important foundation of good practice, and this manual provides a sound basis for helping supervisors develop the skills they need to do their job to the best of their ability.

Who is this manual for?

Actual and aspiring supervisors and leaders and those involved in training and supporting them would be the obvious answer, perhaps. This would include:

▶ team leaders or team managers or others involved in supervising and leading groups of staff (section heads, for example)

▶ senior managers, both operational and strategic

▶ staff in personnel or human resources teams who are responsible for advising others on supervision and leadership matters

▶ councillors, trustees, directors and others involved in policy development, implementation and review

▶ anyone involved in practice learning – supervisors of students on placement, and mentors and/or assessors of colleagues undertaking in-service qualifications.

The manual will be of value in a wide range of organisations across the private, public and voluntary sectors. It is perhaps inevitable that, at times, the authors' public service background will be apparent, but this should not detract from the fact that supervision is an important issue across all organisations, regardless of sector or type.

We envisage the manual being used by two main groups of people whose duties include organising and running training courses, workshops and seminars. The first is likely to comprise in-house training and development staff, such as training managers, staff development officers and so on. The second is likely to comprise those who provide training services on a commercial basis, whether individual freelance trainers or employees or associates of commercial training provider companies.

Introduction

What is supervision?

Literally, the term 'supervision' refers to the process of 'watching over'. However, we should not see it too literally as a process of 'keeping an eye on' staff. The reality of supervision is far more complex than that.

Supervision is basically the process organisations use to manage the relationship between the overall organisation and its needs on the one hand, and the individual and his or her needs on the other. Sometimes the two sets of needs are compatible, but at other times there may be a degree of conflict or tension. The supervisor's task can therefore be seen as: (i) helping to make the most of those aspects of working life where the individual and the organisation are 'on the same wavelength' and a lot of progress can be achieved (for example, where the organisation's need for high-quality practice overlaps with the individual staff member's need for job satisfaction); (ii) managing the tension between the organisation and the individual where there isn't such an overlap (for example, where a new policy may be resisted because one or more members of staff disapprove of it or an aspect of it).

The specific tasks involved, and their importance, should become clearer in the pages that follow.

What is reflective supervision?

Professor Eileen Munro, in her review of the UK child protection system (Munro, 2011), argued the case for supervision to be *reflective* – that is, more than simply a process of reviewing cases. It should be an opportunity to think carefully about key issues, weigh up decisions, draw on our professional knowledge base, promote learning, review practices and basically create a space for reflective practice. Thompson (2018a) explains reflective practice in the following terms:

'I have often been asked on training courses I have run about reflective practice how I would characterize reflective practice in one sentence, and my reply would always be the same: "You've got a brain, use it". A fuller definition would be:

Reflective practice is intelligent, thoughtful practice informed by professional knowledge, skills and values.'

(p111)

We can therefore understand reflective supervision as a form of supervision that draws on, reinforces and develops professional knowledge, skills and values. This is precisely the type of supervision that this manual seeks to support.

How to use this manual

This manual has been designed to help support people who are seeking to help develop standards of supervision. It provides a foundation for running training courses, carrying out staff development activities and planning teaching sessions as part of a college or university programme of learning.

We suggest that, to begin with, you read through the manual quite quickly in order to get an overview of the ideas discussed and the approach adopted. Once you have familiarised yourself with the text in this way, you will then be in a strong position to work your way slowly and thoroughly through the manual, step by step, making sure that you have got to grips with each section before moving on to the next one. In this way you will steadily develop a solid foundation of understanding on which to base your work in relation to developing the role of leader. Once you have completed this second, more demanding reading of the manual, your work is still not over! You will need to refer back to the manual from time to time (perhaps quite frequently at first until you get used to using it) as a point of reference.

The manual is specifically designed to be used in a threefold way:

1. A general introduction and overview – which for many will be an invaluable boost to confidence before planning and running training events.

2. A fairly detailed guide to planning and running training courses and staff development sessions on supervision skills.

3. A reference resource to be consulted as and when required.

Effective supervision pays dividends for all concerned in terms of:

▶ higher standards of work

▶ higher levels of job satisfaction

▶ better working environment or 'climate'

▶ fewer mistakes or difficult situations to deal with

▶ clearer procedures and expectations

▶ more and better opportunities for learning.

This manual can therefore play an important role in helping you develop your knowledge and skills in promoting staff development and therefore, indirectly, higher standards of practice and better outcomes.

Structure

The manual is divided into three main parts. Following this introductory section, Part One is entitled 'Setting the context', and that is precisely what it sets out to do. It discusses the importance of staff development in general and supervision in particular, emphasising how important effective supervision can be across a wide range of organisations. The information provided here should serve to (i) provide a good foundation of knowledge to boost confidence before staging learning events around supervision issues and (ii) provide food for thought to promote further learning and development of these important but complex issues.

Part Two provides a set of training exercises that can be used directly by following the guidance given or can be adapted for use in different ways by trainers or tutors who are confident and experienced enough to do this. The exercises are clearly laid out for ease of reference during an actual learning session.

Part Three contains the conclusion – a summary of the main themes and issues underpinning the manual, together with suggestions for further reading and details of relevant organisations and relevant internet resources. It is important that this part should not be seen simply as an add on. We want to emphasise that supervision is a complex matter that is sadly often oversimplified. The deeper and broader our understanding of supervision, the stronger a position we are in to help establish the highest possible quality of supervision.

> **Disclaimer**
>
> This manual has been researched, prepared and presented in good faith, with all due care and attention. However, no responsibility can be taken for any errors or oversights.
>
> The manual and its contents are intended as a resource to facilitate training and staff development and should not be seen as a definitive statement of employment law. The manual is not a substitute for professional legal advice or guidance and should not be relied upon as such.

Part One:
Setting the context

Reflective supervision

At root, supervision comes down to managers using their knowledge and skills to help get the best out of people on an individual basis. This is why there are strong parallels between supervision and leadership (see the 'Guide to Further Learning' section for details of the *Developing Leadership* manual that parallels this resource). Leadership is concerned with getting the best out of people at a collective level – for example, teams, divisions or even entire organisations. Supervision follows a similar course, but is concerned primarily with getting the best out of individuals. In some ways, then, supervision and leadership are two sides of the same coin.

Unfortunately, some people have a very narrow view of supervision. They see it simply as an administrative process for making sure that staff are doing their job properly. This is highly problematic for various reasons, not least the following:

1. It tends to create tensions and invite a defensive approach on the part of the supervisee. This can lead to game playing and avoidance behaviour. Good reflective supervision should build a relationship based on trust and respect, whereas this type of supervisory relationship is likely to have the opposite effect – that is, it will undermine trust and respect.

2. It comes to be seen as a one-way bureaucratic process, rather than a two-way professional one. It discourages creativity and ownership and is likely to encourage too great a degree of dependency, in the sense that defensive workers are more prone to want to follow instructions than they are to use their professional skills to look for ways forward.

3. It neglects the other (vitally important) aspects of supervision (to be discussed below), leaving supervision one-sided and thus unbalanced. By contrast, where there is due emphasis on the more positive aspects of supervision, there are likely to be far fewer performance issues to be addressed.

4. It makes supervision an unappealing process and is therefore likely to demotivate staff and discourage them from becoming fully involved.

A key part of supervision training therefore needs to be an emphasis on moving away from this narrow perspective of supervision. Our own approach is to stress that supervision is concerned with 'the minimum and the maximum'. By this we mean that it is an important part of supervision to make sure that supervisees are 'doing their job properly' – that is, that they are achieving at least minimum standards of work (in terms of both quantity and quality) and are operating within the appropriate parameters (legal and policy requirements, ethical and professional limits, and so on). However, this is only one part of the equation – this minimum also needs to be counterbalanced by giving due attention to the maximum. By this we mean focusing on fulfilling potential and achieving the best results possible in the circumstances. This wider focus on the maximum as well as the minimum enables supervision to be a positive, empowering and motivating process that staff look forward to, rather than a dry administrative process that they just tolerate, or even dread.

It is important, then, that as you read on about supervision, you try to understand it in this context of being concerned with the minimum and the maximum.

Litmus test

Do supervisees look forward to supervision? If not, this is telling you that it is not fulfilling its potential for creating a reflective and supportive space.

We shall begin by exploring the important role of supervision in ensuring that staff are as fully equipped as possible to undertake their duties, in so far as:

► they are clear about what is expected of them

► they are enabled to learn from their experiences in order to keep abreast of developments and new demands

► they are adequately supported to ensure that the pressures of the work are manageable and not a source of harmful stress.

We shall approach the topic of supervision by seeing it in its broader context – that of 'human resource development' (that is, those interpersonal and organisational processes that contribute to developing – and thus maximising the effectiveness of – the workforce). Again, there is a parallel here with leadership, in so far as both are concerned with:

► keeping a clear focus on the goals we are trying to achieve

► motivating staff to achieve optimal outcomes and maximise their own potential

► contributing to a positive and constructive working environment

► seeking to ensure that staff's contributions are recognised and valued.

What is 'Human resource development'?

Professional responsibility: more than a job

Acting as a line manager involves not only making sure staff carry out their duties to at least a satisfactory standard (minimum), but also helping them to continue learning, developing and building on their existing strengths (maximum). Consequently, it can be helpful to think of the line manager's work under three headings:

► *Knowledge:* In order to work effectively, there are certain things staff need to know. This will vary from job to job, but anything beyond the simplest of manual tasks involves some form of knowledge base.

▶ *Skills:* Staff are expected to develop a range of skills, including interpersonal skills, stress management skills and practical skills. The expectation is not that staff should be experts, but they should be able to develop a range of skills to at least a basic standard of competence.

▶ *Values:* Underpinning the work undertaken by managers and staff will be a set of values, beliefs and assumptions that shape how we think and act. For example, in a retail setting, customer service is an important value to uphold. Without paying attention to such a value, it is unlikely that a retail business will thrive.

It is these three sets of factors that can make someone's work more than a job – elevating it to a vocation or profession that requires certain standards and brings with it certain rewards (see 'Job Satisfaction' below). The question of professional responsibility is therefore an important one and not something that should be taken lightly. In view of this, human resource development has to be seen as a vitally important issue, in so far as it has an essential role to play in terms of ensuring that staff are:

▶ aware of what their roles, tasks, duties and responsibilities are

▶ well informed, well equipped and competent to do their job

▶ kept up to date with developments in theory, practice, policy and law

▶ motivated to do a good job and continue learning

▶ confident but not complacent

▶ learning from their mistakes and from their achievements

▶ able to support each other

▶ able to enjoy their work and gain job satisfaction, and motivated and equipped to take on new challenges.

Use of self

A commonly used term in the helping professions is 'use of self'. This refers to the fact that each individual has much to offer in terms of his or her own personality, experience, relationship skills and so on. Acting as a line manager is a complex business that can test our personal resources: our resilience, patience, calmness, maturity, clear thinking and ability to work under pressure. All this involves use of self. In many occupations – particularly those that involve direct contact with people – use of self is also an important strength for staff to draw upon.

Consequently, the development of self through training and supervision is an important means of increasing effectiveness, reducing the number of mistakes made and increasing job satisfaction. Training and supervision can also play an important role in 'protecting' self. That is, staff development can help to improve stress management skills and help to ensure that staff are not harmed by the emotional pressures that come with many forms of work, reflecting the importance of what has come to be known as emotional intelligence and the related idea of 'emotional labour'.

The significant part played by use of self means that workforce development amounts to more than gaining basic knowledge and technical skills. If staff are to develop their potential to the full, there needs to be an understanding of the importance of use of self and opportunities for building on strengths and overcoming weaknesses. Workforce development and personal development are closely intertwined.

Responsibility for learning

There are often many people involved in the process of learning: tutors, training officers, line managers, colleagues and so on. However, the most important person in all this is the individual learner – unless we take responsibility for our own learning, unless we are committed to developing our understanding and changing the way we think and act, learning will not take place (see the discussion of self-directed learning in Thompson, 2019a).

Although the others involved in the process can facilitate, support or encourage learning, they cannot make learning happen – it is only the individual who can do that ('You can lead a horse to water …'). Consequently, every member of staff has responsibility for his or her own learning.

For staff who have supervisory duties, the responsibility is twofold:

1. Being responsible for the supervision of others does not remove responsibility for one's own learning. No one, no matter how skilled or experienced they may be, ever reaches the point where they have nothing further to learn. Indeed, the attitude of 'I know everything I need to know' is a potentially very dangerous one (see Lifelong learning on p18).

2. Supervisory staff also have some degree of responsibility for facilitating and supporting the learning of the staff they supervise. This relates to both the specific examples of learning that arise in the process of supervision and the general duty to contribute to creating an atmosphere and working environment in which learning is welcomed, encouraged and rewarded (see Making supervision work on p21).

Arguing that people are responsible for their own learning is not a means of 'passing the buck' – for example, by blaming poor quality training on the people who attended the course rather than the person(s) who ran it. It is, however, a necessary acknowledgement of the fact that people will not learn unless they are committed to doing so – unless they take the necessary steps to make it happen. Human resource development, then, is not just a matter of providing training courses – it is a much broader matter that involves:

▶ creating the right atmosphere for learning – relaxed and friendly, but not complacent or without challenge

▶ supporting staff in their attempts to learn and develop their knowledge, skills and values

▶ recognising, encouraging and using opportunities for learning

▶ dealing with mistakes constructively rather than negatively.

It is also important to note that learning involves a process of change. If we are still the same after a learning experience, then what was the point of learning? Learning involves moving on, developing a new perspective and gaining new knowledge and/ or skills. Because of this process of change at the heart of learning, it can sometimes be a painful process that involves letting go of things which we have perhaps taken for granted for a very long time (a lot of learning about values and equality and diversity involves this type of 'letting go' or 'unlearning' – see Equality and Diversity below). We should therefore be honest and acknowledge that learning can sometimes be difficult and demanding, reflecting the old saying: 'There's no gain without pain'.

Equality and diversity

In order to promote equality and affirm diversity, it is necessary to encourage approaches to work that:

▶ are not based on prejudice or discrimination against particular individuals, groups or categories of people

▶ do not condone or reinforce existing inequalities – for example, by relying on stereotypes

▶ challenge the discriminatory or oppressive actions and attitudes of others

▶ recognise that we live in a 'diverse' society – that is, one where people come from many different backgrounds – and that we should not regard differences between people as problems or weaknesses.

We must therefore pay attention to basic questions of equality of opportunity in order to ensure that staff are able to develop their knowledge and skills in ways that are consistent with the value base. This includes the following:

▶ recognising the importance of each individual's cultural background or heritage and respecting his or her customs, practices, choice of food and so on

▶ acknowledging the experience of disadvantage and oppression by certain groups and individuals as a result of racism, sexism, disablism and so on, and developing sensitivity to the ways in which stereotypes and unquestioned assumptions can reinforce inequality and disadvantage – for example, by assuming that people with disabilities cannot make decisions for themselves.

Consequently, equality of opportunity and the potential for discrimination need to be recurring themes within our human resource development efforts. These issues are discussed in more detail in the *Learning from Practice* manual *Promoting Equality, Valuing Diversity* (Thompson, 2019b).

Lifelong learning

Reflective practice

One of the dangers associated with working life is the potential for developing 'routinised practice', a way of working characterised by unthinking routines where we are operating on 'automatic pilot'. This is a dangerous form of practice because:

▶ important aspects of a situation may not be recognised because the uniqueness of each set of circumstances may not be appreciated

▶ the wrong approach may be used – trying to fit a square peg into a round hole

▶ customers, service users or other important stakeholders may get the impression that their specific needs or circumstances are not being taken into consideration, that they are not valued or important

▶ creativity and the use of imaginative approaches are stifled

▶ opportunities for gaining job satisfaction are limited (see below).

This is not to say that routines have no place in working life – clearly they do. A set of routines can be a significant source of a sense of security, a sense of 'rhythm' and familiarity. Routines are also important ways of saving time and energy by undertaking repetitive tasks in as efficient a way as possible. However, an important skill is that of being able to distinguish between when a routine is appropriate and harmless, and when such a routine would be inappropriate and therefore dangerous. That is, we have to recognise that many things cannot be safely dealt with as a matter of routine.

Job satisfaction

Working with people makes various demands upon us, but also brings many rewards. It is important to recognise that job satisfaction is like a form of fuel that keeps us going. Without it, there is a danger that we may get worn down, lacking in energy, motivation or commitment. And this can be the beginning of a vicious circle. If we don't get job satisfaction, if we don't get the necessary rewards and satisfactions from our work, we are less likely to be effective or to work with flair and imagination, because we are less highly motivated, less likely to be 'on top form'.

If we are not motivated and committed to what we are doing, we are much less likely to achieve any job satisfaction – a circle has been set up, a vicious circle in which two destructive aspects (low job satisfaction and low standards of practice) reinforce each other, thereby increasing the destructive potential of the situation. Consequently, job satisfaction has to be seen as a key issue in maintaining high standards of practice.

Human resource development has a part to play in maintaining and enhancing levels of job satisfaction. This applies in a number of ways:

- by encouraging staff to reflect on their practice and appreciate achievements gained, progress made and lessons learned

- by developing confidence and skills

- by providing a wider range of options to draw on

- by providing a sense of achievement, progress and direction.

Keeping up to date

Working life is not 'static'. That is, situations change, new circumstances arise, new developments occur, things move on. For example, a new development in one's work brings a fresh set of challenges, a new set of issues to address. Consequently, staff have a duty to keep up to date with such developments. These include:

- new ideas that can improve practice

- changes in policy or procedures

- changes in the law or statutory guidance

- learning from new research or other developments in the knowledge base.

This does not mean that staff have to have their noses in books for long periods of time. It does, however, mean that – for many grades of staff, at least – there is an expectation that some effort is made to read about new developments, to share ideas and help keep one another up to date.

Keeping up to date with important developments should not be seen as a chore, but rather as a fairly normal activity as part of the overall process of staff development. In this way it becomes part of 'lifelong learning' as well as a further potential source of job satisfaction.

Investing in people

Cost or investment?

Staff are usually the most expensive resource in an organisation. That is, the costs of maintaining a workforce usually exceed any other costs the organisation has to bear. This is particularly the case in the helping professions, where people's skills, knowledge and commitment are so vitally important. However, there is a danger in seeing the situation mainly in terms of costs. A more helpful approach is to think of the money spent on staff as an investment, rather than simply a set of costs.

Human resource development involves a considerable investment of time, effort, energy and money. However, the benefits to be gained from an effective system of staff development can outweigh these costs. These benefits should not be underestimated, because they:

▶ are an important aspect of having a well-informed, confident and committed group of staff

▶ create a positive working environment in which staff feel valued and supported

▶ reduce the chances of costly mistakes being made

▶ enhance the reputation and standing of the organisation

▶ improve levels of service and the quality of life of customers, service users and so on.

It is therefore important to recognise that developing staff is an essential investment in good practice rather than simply a drain on the organisation's resources.

Staff care

It has long been recognised that working life has the potential to be very stressful. It involves a number of pressures that can, if they are not dealt with appropriately, cause considerable harm. These pressures include:

▶ the physical demands of the various tasks associated with many jobs – not just manual jobs, but also a wide range of posts that can be physically demanding

▶ the risk of encountering aggression and violence in some situations – sadly not as uncommon an occurrence as we might like to think

▶ the emotional demands that arise as a result of the potential conflicts and tensions involved in various work settings – whether in public service or the commercial world

▶ the risk of getting things wrong and doing harm instead of good – something that can apply in any form of work.

Dealing with stress is partly an individual responsibility, but not entirely so. Organisations also have a degree of responsibility for ensuring that their staff are not exposed to excessive levels of pressure. In some ways, this is a reflection of health and safety responsibilities, and is partly a question of good management practice in ensuring that there is an ethos of 'staff care' as part of a commitment to workplace well-being.

Staff care is a term that refers to the various steps that employers can or do take to promote the well-being of their staff, so that they are able to fulfil their duties effectively and gain satisfaction from doing so. These steps include induction, supervision, appraisal, grievance procedures, maternity leave and, of course, training and staff development (guidance on each of these is to be found in Thompson, 2013).

Human resource development is a key element in the overall process of staff care, and staff care, in turn, is an important part of investing in people.

Healthy organisations

Some organisations work in such a way that they have a very detrimental effect on their staff. Work is an important part of people's lives, and so problems or tensions at work can have a very significant effect on our health and well-being. No organisation will be perfect or ideally suited to staff, but some are certainly much better than others when it comes to providing a positive environment in which to work.

One of the things that can be associated with organisations that cause undue problems for their staff is a failure to support staff in developing the knowledge, skills and values necessary to carry out the work successfully and satisfyingly. A 'healthy' organisation is therefore one that, among other things, provides the necessary backing for staff to carry out their duties effectively and gain job satisfaction from doing so. A key part of this backing that an organisation must provide is an appropriate system of staff development, which:

▶ continuously provides opportunities for learning

▶ encourages learning

▶ discourages defensiveness and allows people to be open about their learning needs without fear of undue criticism

▶ continues to make staff development a priority, even though this may be difficult at times due to other pressures.

Making supervision work

What is supervision?

We have already noted that, literally, the term 'supervision' refers to the process of 'watching over'. However, the reality of supervision is, or should be, far more complex than that. It should involve different elements of helping the supervisee to be the best, most effective worker they can be (minimum and maximum again).

It is essential that we move beyond the idea that supervision is a one-way bureaucratic process of controlling an employee. We need to see it as a reflective two-way professional process. By two-way, we mean that the supervisee needs to be an active partner (in agenda setting, for example), rather than a passive recipient of instructions. By professional, we mean geared towards developing knowledge and skills through reflective practice, rather than 'plateauing' (that is, improving initially but soon flattening out in terms of development).

Who is the supervisor responsible for?

This is a question we cannot answer directly. We have raised the question because it is vitally important that supervisors are aware of which particular members of staff they are responsible for in terms of development. This is a particularly important responsibility, in so far as it involves sharing responsibility for other people's work in terms of standards of practice (accountability), support (staff care) and learning (staff development). These are discussed in more detail below. The bottom line, however, is that, if something goes wrong for a supervisee, the supervisor will share some degree of responsibility for the situation.

In view of the fact that supervisory responsibilities are so important, it is essential that supervisors are completely clear about which members of staff they are responsible for. In supervising staff who are themselves supervisors (either of other staff or of students on placement), it will be necessary to ensure that they too are taking their supervisory responsibilities seriously.

Of course, another important factor to consider is: who is responsible for supervising you? Clear expectations about the nature of supervisory relationships and their implications are an important part of a healthy organisation. However, this is a two-way process. If the system is to work smoothly and to maximum effect, it is important that supervisors and supervisees work co-operatively together. Supervisors therefore need to consider not one set of issues but two:

1. How can I make sure that my supervision of staff is as good as it possibly can be?

2. How can I make the best possible use of the supervision I receive? What are my supervisor's responsibilities?

Supervisory responsibilities can be divided into four 'elements' or categories: accountability, staff care, staff development and mediation.

Accountability

Organisations usually work on the basis that supervisors are accountable for the actions of their staff. That is, where basic-grade staff act in a particular way, the supervisor concerned shares some degree of responsibility for those actions – this is the basis of accountability. Consequently, it is very important that supervisors recognise their responsibility for others. If this doesn't happen, there is a very real danger that the errors of staff will backfire on their supervisors. And, ironically, if supervisory staff are not taking their accountability role seriously, the likelihood of mistakes being made is that much higher, as opportunities to 'nip them in the bud' will be missed.

Staff care

The importance of staff care has already been emphasised. Supervisory staff have a very important role to play in terms of making sure that staff feel valued and adequately supported. A supportive line manager is a major benefit for a staff member, whereas an unsupportive one can be a source of resentment and ill feeling. Staff care plays an important role in helping staff fend off stress and its harmful effects on health, relationships, standards of work and so on.

Staff development

A common misunderstanding of supervision is that it is primarily, if not exclusively, about accountability (and therefore often referred to disparagingly as 'snoopervision').

The responsibility for helping staff learn and develop is one that is often neglected in many organisations. This is partly because many supervisors feel uncomfortable with the role. They are much happier with a managerial accountability role and don't feel very happy addressing people's learning needs or helping to remove barriers to learning. However, as this manual should be making perfectly clear, staff development is a crucial part of the work of anyone with supervisory responsibilities.

Mediation

Sometimes it is necessary to act as a 'mediator' between one or more members of staff that you supervise and other parts of the organisation, or even people outside the organisation – for example, in multidisciplinary working. For example, a member of staff may have a grievance against the organisation and may need your support to get the matter resolved. This role is sometimes referred to as 'fighting up, selling down' – that is, representing the interests of staff (fighting up) has to be balanced against representing the organisation (selling down or 'cooling out'). Handling this tension (and keeping both sides happy) is a very skilled job and needs to be taken very seriously. If supervisors neglect the staff they supervise, they will encounter resentment and mistrust, thereby making their job very difficult. If, on the other hand, they act against the interests of the organisation, they could again be making their job a lot harder by creating conflict between themselves and the employer – and this too could backfire on staff.

Why should I bother?

There are various reasons why supervisors should not adopt a 'Why bother?' attitude, not least of which is the fact that they would not be doing their job properly! However, one particularly important reason is what can be called the 'doubling' effect. Look at it this way: if you play an active part in staff development, you will be contributing positively to standards of practice, levels of skill and knowledge, motivation, job satisfaction and so on. However, where staff development issues are neglected or discouraged, the net result can be one of resentment, ill feeling and mistrust – all of which can undermine confidence, motivation and quality of work. The difference between the two is therefore double (see Figure 1).

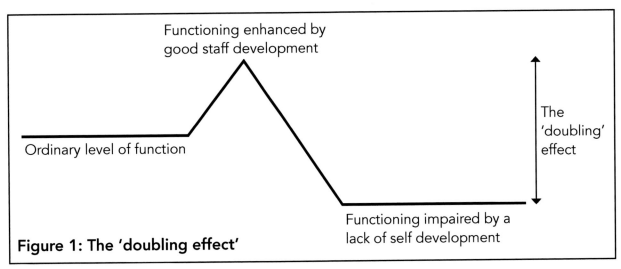

Figure 1: The 'doubling effect'

Troubleshooting

Resistance and non-cooperation

Sometimes staff members do not understand or appreciate the nature or importance of staff development. Similarly, some people may feel threatened by staff development – they may see it as something that may reveal their weaknesses or undermine their confidence (this can apply in relation to both training courses and supervision). For others it may simply be a question of fear of the unknown. But whatever the reason, the outcome is likely to be resistance and/or a lack of co-operation – in other words, serious obstacles to learning. Consequently, it is important that strategies are developed to counteract such resistance sensitively and constructively. These can include:

▶ *Talking things through:* Often anxieties, misconceptions and other barriers to learning can be removed by 'talking them through', either in supervision or more informally.

▶ *Naming the process:* Where someone is displaying resistance, for example by changing the subject whenever certain issues are raised, it can be very effective to 'name the process', to state explicitly what is happening: 'There you go again, you're changing the subject' – see Thompson (2012).

▶ *Sticking with it:* It is not uncommon for people to show some degree of resistance initially, but then begin to warm to the idea and settle down. It's therefore important not to overreact and start tackling the issues too soon. They will often sort themselves out fairly quickly.

Conflicts

There may well be times when the supervisor and a staff member do not see eye to eye, when personal differences get in the way of good working relations. This can cause serious difficulties in terms of a positive atmosphere for learning. Such a conflict can cause great tension – tension that prevents positive learning. Consequently, there is a need for staff with supervisory responsibilities to take steps to ensure that such clashes are avoided or their effects minimised. These include:

▶ *Assertiveness:* Finding a helpful balance between being submissive and being domineering can help to keep conflicts to a minimum or avoid them altogether.

▶ *Unconditional positive regard:* This is an idea put forward by Carl Rogers (1961). It means that we should adopt a positive attitude towards the people we are trying to help, regardless of who they are or what they may have done. In this context, it would involve putting any personal feelings to one side and maintaining a positive professional working relationship.

▶ *Clearing the air:* Sometimes the tensions between people can become so great that it is necessary to 'clear the air' – to address the situation directly. This does not have to involve confrontation, but it does mean being prepared to discuss differences openly, honestly and constructively.

▶ *Third party support:* At times it may become necessary to involve a third person to help resolve difficulties, to act as a 'mediator'. This is a relatively rare occurrence but, if used sensitively, can be a turning point in a difficult relationship or situation.

NB Although conflicts can cause a lot of problems, it should be remembered that the relationship between staff is, ultimately, a professional one geared towards providing high standards of practice. It is therefore the responsibility of all staff, but supervisory staff in particular, to take all reasonable steps to prevent personal differences from getting in the way of effective practice.

Workload management

The old saying 'you can't fit a quart into a pint pot' has a lot of truth in it. That is, there is only so much work that an individual can do in a given day. Consequently, it is understandable that staff may sometimes claim they are too busy to get involved in staff development activities, or too busy to take the time to reflect on their work and learn from it. However, although it is understandable, it is still a problem that needs to be addressed and resolved.

It is therefore very important to take seriously the question of workload management.

In view of the importance of staff development in terms of motivation, job satisfaction and standards of work, it really is a false economy to neglect staff development because we are 'too busy'. This is parallelled with the driver who is too busy to have his or her car serviced or maintained and then finds that a great deal of time is wasted when it breaks down.

Staff can be helped, encouraged and supported in managing their workload effectively so that staff development does not get pushed to one side by other pressures. This can be done in a variety of ways, including the following:

▶ *Setting priorities:* 'First things first' is an important motto. When people are busy or under pressure it is relatively easy to lose track of priorities. When this happens there is a danger that very important things are not done while less important matters receive attention. A clear focus on priorities is therefore an important part of staff development.

▶ *Maintaining motivation:* Managing a workload is not just a question of managing time; it also involves managing levels of energy and motivation. If staff are keen and motivated, they will achieve a lot more than if they are feeling bored, unstimulated or generally lacking in motivation. This brings us back to the key issue of job satisfaction discussed above.

▶ *Reviewing work regularly:* An important part of workload management is having a sense of control. A sense of control reduces anxiety and increases confidence, motivation and clarity of purpose. Regular reviews of work tasks (to measure progress and identify what remains to be done) can play a very important part in developing and maintaining that sense of control.

What about the supervisor's development?

Responsibility for learning

The point was emphasised earlier that learning is primarily the task of the learner. This applies not only when supporting other people in their learning, but also in managing and developing our own learning. We therefore have to be clear about what steps are being taken to ensure that supervisors are learning too. It is very easy for people who are concerned with the learning of others to neglect their own – to get wrapped up in helping others without helping themselves. Being responsible for supporting the learning and development of others does not take away the responsibility for our own learning.

The learning organisation

The notion of the 'learning organisation' is an important one. A learning organisation, as the name implies, makes learning a priority. As Roderick put it some time ago, learning organisations:

- ▶ *'take every opportunity to learn both from experience and in general at individual, group and corporate level*

- ▶ *experiment with new ways of organising work and new ways of learning both within and outside the organisation*

- ▶ *establish a climate in which learning from each other is actively supported*

- ▶ *use the training function to facilitate the development and learning of all employees*

- ▶ *see a key role for managers as facilitators*

- ▶ *develop structures which encourage two-way communication as a means of promoting learning and development*

- ▶ *encourage questioning, experimentation and exploration of new ideas at all levels*

- ▶ *remove barriers and blockages to learning in both the individual and the environment*

- ▶ *encourage and foster continuous learning and self-development in all employees*

- ▶ *think about how to learn as well as what to learn.'*

(1993, p13)

All employees, especially those with supervisory responsibilities, have an important part to play in building and maintaining a learning organisation. In pursuing their own staff development as well as supporting others, they are contributing to the development of a learning organisation.

Part of the solution or part of the problem?

In making a positive contribution to staff development, supervisors take steps towards achieving positive outcomes and increased levels of job satisfaction. If, however, they do not make such a positive contribution, they may be undermining quality of work and job satisfaction. This is because, in neglecting the staff development role, we are contributing to the problem rather than the solution – we are giving the impression that unthinking, uncritical practice is acceptable, that it is not necessary for staff to learn and develop. There is a responsibility for supervisory staff to 'set a good example' by taking very seriously their own learning needs and doing something positive about them. We cannot expect staff to demonstrate a commitment to staff development and lifelong learning if their supervisors do not do the same.

Conclusion

Being committed to ongoing development can be a major strength of any organisation. In order to make the most of that strength, we feel very strongly that staff development must be undertaken in partnership. It requires a commitment from all concerned if high standards are to be achieved and maintained. This involves contributing the time, effort, energy and vision required for:

▶ *Supervisors:* to support staff in their learning and to ensure that supervision is more than a tokenistic attempt to appear supportive.

▶ *All staff:* to play an active role in continuing to learn and develop, continuously enhancing standards of practice and levels of job satisfaction.

▶ *Senior managers:* to fund and manage staff development and make any changes that become necessary in order to maximise its effectiveness.

This sounds like a major commitment – and indeed it is – but it offers immense rewards in a number of ways. A lack of commitment to staff development, by contrast, is a false economy that has many costs for staff, for the organisation as a whole, but most of all for the people the organisation serves.

Part Two:
The exercises

Introduction

In Part Two of the manual we present a range of exercises. Here you will find details of activities that can be used as the basis of training courses or staff development exercises. Various exercises refer to presentation slides; these are to be found online at www.pavpub.com/learning-from-practice-resources.

The exercises are described in such a way as to be useful to both experienced trainers and those with little or no experience of running training sessions. It is likely that more experienced trainers will want to adapt materials to suit their own purposes and their own styles of working. However, less experienced trainers are more likely to want to follow each of the exercises step by step. We present the materials in this way so that they can be used with maximum flexibility according to need.

A note on timing

Getting the timing right is one of the most difficult and demanding aspects of delivering training or other learning sessions. This is partly because it is so difficult to predict how long different groups will take to complete tasks or how long a discussion will go on for, and partly because different trainers have different styles when it comes to use of the time (some like to press on quickly from one section to another, while others like to approach things more slowly and draw out as much learning as they can).

Being able to manage timings is a skill that develops over time with experience. If you are new to this we suggest you keep an eye on the clock and, if you are over-running at any point, think about possible shortcuts to get you reasonably back on schedule, but try to avoid bringing a good, useful discussion to a premature close if you can. If, on the other hand, you find that you are ahead of schedule and you are concerned about running out of material, there are two things you can do:

1. Consider whether you can extend any part of the remaining material.

2. At a suitable point, invite the group to work in pairs to review the learning so far. After five minutes or so, reconvene the main group and ask for feedback from their discussions. This can then lead into a further discussion that makes very good use of the remaining time.

Most of the exercises in this manual are likely to take between 60 and 80 minutes, which fits well with common timetables for training courses or college and university teaching sessions. However, we recommend that you look closely at the guidance given for each exercise in advance and make your own mind up about how long you want the session to last or how you might want to adapt it to fit the time available. If you feel uncomfortable about this, consult a more experienced colleague who may be able to give you useful guidance. If at all possible, you may find it very helpful to run some of the sessions jointly with a colleague until you feel you have mastered them.

Exercise 1: Experiences of supervision

Aim

This exercise comes in two versions. It can be used either as a straightforward group discussion exercise or at a more advanced level as a guided fantasy.

Materials

Flip chart paper and pens

Blu Tack or masking tape

Timing

All in all, this exercise is likely to take between 70 and 80 minutes.

Introduction: 5 minutes

Groupwork: 25 minutes

Feedback and discussion: 35 minutes

Summary and conclusion: 5 minutes

Activity

For the straightforward version of this exercise the steps to take are as follows:

▶ First, explain to the group that this exercise will enable them to explore their positive and negative experiences of supervision. Next, divide the main group into subgroups of between four and six people. Issue each group with a sheet of flip chart paper and a marker pen. Ask the groups to draw a line down the middle of their flip chart paper and, through group discussion, develop a list of positive experiences, which they should record on the left-hand side of the paper, and negative experiences, which they should record on the right-hand side.

▶ Explain to the groups that, if they complete one side of the flip chart paper, they should ask for a second sheet rather than go over to the other side. This is because the flip chart paper will be displayed on the walls at a later stage in the exercise. Once people have had a chance to explore their ideas and record them on the paper, display the various sheets on the walls around the room. Give each group a few minutes to walk around the room looking at what other groups have come up with and comparing notes. Once they have had the opportunity to digest the range of ideas across the various sheets of flipchart paper, ask the group to reconvene into the main group. Once the group have settled again, use the remaining time to chair a discussion based on the exercise. This should provide a good opportunity to bring out the key points that make for positive supervision and give good guidance as to what negative steps to avoid.

▶ Use the last few minutes of the exercise to sum up the key learning points or ask the group to do so.

For the more advanced version of this exercise replace the time spent in small groups with a guided fantasy exercise. Note that it is not advisable for inexperienced trainers to try this exercise.

▶ A guided fantasy involves asking the participants to close their eyes and relax. Once they are in a suitably quiet and relaxed state, ask them to envisage memories of positive experiences of having been supervised in the recent or distant past; allow two to three minutes for this. Then ask the participants to open their eyes to take a partner, and, while in their pairs, to compare notes of their experiences; allow a few moments for this.

▶ Next, repeat the exercise, but with a focus this time on negative experiences of supervision. Once again, ask the participants to break off into pairs once they have had the opportunity to reflect quietly on negative experiences of supervision. Once you have completed these two elements of guided fantasy, ask the pairs to join up with other pairs in order to form smaller groups. Once they are in their groups, issue a sheet of flip chart paper and pens to each group. Unlike in the first version of this exercise, the participants should not be asked to record their actual positive and negative experiences, but rather should work at a more advanced level to identify the key themes which underpin the positive and negative aspects of supervisory management practice. From here on in, this version of the exercise should follow a similar pattern to the more straightforward version of the exercise described above.

Exercise 2: Induction

Aim

This exercise gives participants the opportunity to prepare an induction package for new staff.

Materials

Flip chart paper and pens or white board and pens

Timing

Between 60 and 80 minutes should be sufficient, but the exercise can be used flexibly.

Activity

▶ Begin by explaining that the object of this exercise is to give participants the opportunity to develop an understanding of what is involved in effective induction. Explain that induction can be crucial in terms of how a new supervisee settles into the team or workgroup, how positive a contribution they can make and how problems can be avoided. In some respects, it can be make or break: it can make someone feel welcome and valued and can thus motivate them and contribute to overall morale. It can also make sure they are clear about their duties, how the organisation works and so on. Poor or non-existent induction, however, can leave new employees feeling confused, disorientated, not welcome, not valued and unclear about how they are expected to fit into the overall scheme of things. They can become demotivated, resentful and stressed as a result of this.

▶ Divide the main group into subgroups of four to six people. Give each subgroup a sheet of flip chart paper and a pen. Ask them to write 'My Ideal Induction' as a heading across the top. Explain that you want them to imagine that they have just started a new job and are about to begin an induction programme. Invite them to record on the flip chart their idea of what would constitute their ideal induction. What would they want to happen? What would they need to know? What 'message' would they want the overall process to give them?

▶ Allow 20 to 25 minutes for this groupwork then reconvene the group. The feedback from the subgroups can then form the basis of a discussion that allows you and the group to pool together all the information to map out what an ideal induction would look like. It can be helpful to ask the group to consider what obstacles might prevent the induction of a new employee from being ideal and what they could do as supervisors to get as close to that ideal as possible.

▶ If you have time, allow about 10 minutes towards the end to draw out what the group regards as the key principles of effective induction.

▶ Use the last few minutes to sum up the lessons learned from the session, or ask the group to do so.

Exercise 3: Preparing for supervision

Aim

In this exercise participants are helped to understand the importance of both parties preparing for a supervision session.

Materials

Flip chart paper and pens or white board and pens

Worksheet 1: Preparing for supervision

Timing

60 to 80 minutes should be sufficient for this activity.

Activity

▶ Begin by explaining to the group that you are going to be working together on developing a clearer picture of how preparation can allow you to get the best out of a supervision session. Make it clear that supervision should be seen as 'quality time' and should therefore be used as wisely as possible, and that careful preparation – by both supervisor and supervisee – can be very helpful in this regard.

▶ Next, divide the main group into subgroups of four to six people and give each member a copy of **Worksheet 1: Preparing for supervision**. Explain that they will now have 20 to 25 minutes to help one another complete the worksheet and come up with an overall picture of what sort of preparations can be useful.

▶ When you are ready, reconvene the main group and begin a plenary feedback and discussion session. Divide the feedback into three parts. First, focus on what the supervisee can do by way of preparation; second, consider what the supervisor can do; and finally, ask each group if they were able to identify any conclusions that can be drawn from the exercise (as the worksheet invites them to do). As each point is made, encourage the group to expand on why they think this is important (this is to prevent a fairly mechanistic feedback process and to encourage a helpful discussion about the value of preparation and the specific steps that can be taken).

▶ Use the last few minutes to sum up the learning or invite the group to do so.

Please note that the following issues are likely to occur. If any of them do not, you can weave them into the discussion:

▶ *Arranging an appropriate venue*

This is to ensure no interruptions or distractions.

▶ *Undertaking pre-supervision reading*

If you need (or they want you) to read a file or report to be discussed in supervision, make sure you receive it in plenty of time so that you are not wasting supervision time reading materials that could have been read beforehand.

▶ *Agenda setting*

This is best done as a shared exercise to make sure that both parties' issues are covered. This process should also include a discussion of agenda item priorities to make sure that you do not run out of time before discussing crucial issues.

▶ *Planning*

Agenda setting can take far less time if both parties have planned beforehand what they want to cover in the session. It is wise for both supervisor and supervisee to make notes in between sessions so that they are well informed about what they see as important issues and do not lose track of them between one session and the next.

▶ *Comfort needs*

If you are going to have a drink while you talk, make sure that this is sorted out before you start and that you are not wasting valuable supervision time while you wait for the kettle to boil. Similarly, try to make sure that toilet visits occur before or after, not during. Protect the quality time.

Worksheet 1: Preparing for supervision

What preparatory steps can be taken to help make the most of the time available for supervision?

By the supervisee

By you as supervisor

What conclusions might you be able to draw from this exercise?

Exercise 4: Beginnings and endings

Aim

This exercise helps participants to appreciate the significance of good beginnings and good endings.

Materials

Flip chart paper and pens or white board and pens

Slide 1: Beginnings and endings

Worksheet 2: Beginnings and endings

Timing

Allow 60 to 80 minutes.

Activity

▶ Begin by explaining to the group that this exercise will help them understand why it is important to get a supervision session off to a good start and to finish well. Follow this with a short presentation (say, 15 minutes) about the reasons behind this (use **Slide 1: Beginnings and endings**). Invite comments and questions about what you have covered (or what you are covering, if you are happy to be interrupted – some less experienced presenters find it hard to retain their flow if they are interrupted).

▶ After you are happy that the group have understood the key points, divide them into subgroups of four to six and give each participant a copy of **Worksheet 2: Beginnings and endings**. Invite them to help each other fill in their worksheet by identifying what they see as DOs and DON'Ts in relation to both beginnings and endings. How long to leave for this will depend on how much time you have allocated for this section, but we would suggest a minimum of 15 minutes and a maximum of 25. Make it clear that your presentation has laid the foundations by offering them general principles, and they are now being asked to take this further by identifying specific steps to take (DOs) or avoid (DON'Ts). When you are ready, reconvene the main group and begin a plenary feedback and discussion session. Try to ensure that the session identifies key learning points (perhaps recording these on the whiteboard or flip chart as you come up with them) to make sure the session is not just a dry (and potentially boring) reporting-back session.

▶ Leave some time towards the end to sum up the main learning points or invite the group to do so. Finally, invite the group to reflect and comment on how they feel the session has gone in terms of how it started (make sure you start it well!) and how best to end it. This can be both a fun ending and a good learning point or set of learning points.

Worksheet 2: Beginnings and endings

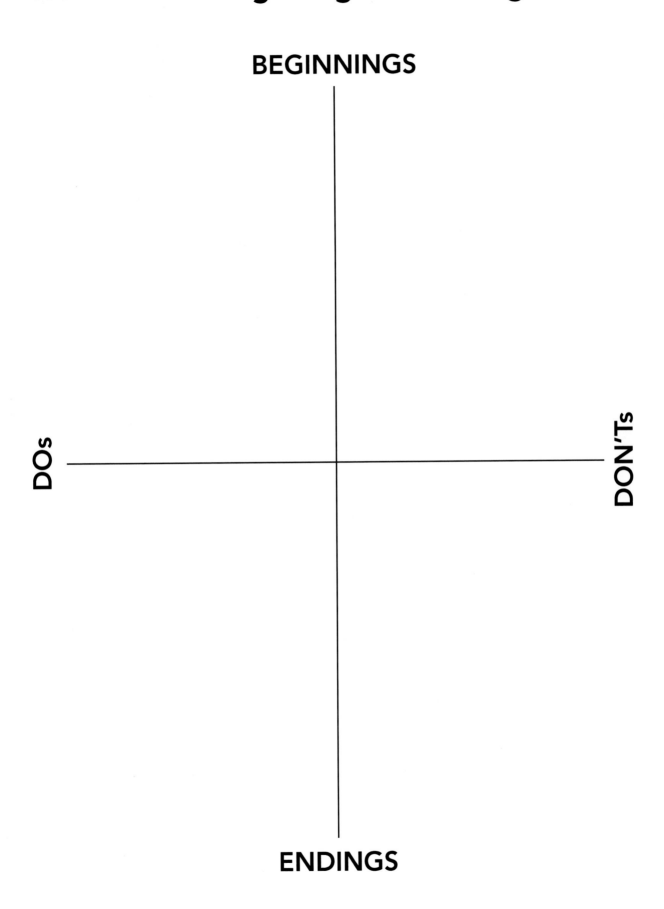

BEGINNINGS

DOs

DON'Ts

ENDINGS

Exercise 5: Giving feedback

Aim

This exercise involves a short presentation using Slide 2, followed by a skill rehearsal session.

Materials

Flip chart paper and pens or white board and pens

Slide 2: Giving feedback

Worksheet 3: Giving feedback

Timing

This exercise is likely to take 80 minutes.

Presentation based on Slide 2: 15 minutes

Exercise in trios: 35 minutes

Feedback and conclusion: 25 minutes

Summary: 5 minutes

Activity

▶ Begin the session by explaining to the group that this exercise is geared towards exploring how best to give feedback to supervisees. It recognises that the skills involved in giving feedback can be crucial in terms of forming a positive working relationship. Supervisees can gain great reassurance from knowing that they will be given a balance of positive and negative feedback on their performance, so it is important that effective supervisors are able to use feedback as a constructive tool. These comments should be incorporated into an introduction to the exercise, and the opportunity should also be taken to explain to participants that in this activity they will have the opportunity not only to talk about feedback skills, but also to practice them.

▶ Next, using **Slide 2: Giving feedback**, present to the group the key points about good practice in using feedback constructively. Go through each heading on Slide 2 slowly and carefully, making sure that participants fully understand the points being made. Where possible, give an example of each of the points on the sheet or board. Participants may have questions at this stage, and it is quite appropriate to respond to these now. However, you should resist the temptation to get involved in a detailed discussion at this point. This will work better towards the end of the session after people have had the opportunity to practice the skills concerned.

▶ Next, divide the group into trios. Ask each person within the trio to adopt the letter A, B or C. Subsequently explain to the group that, to begin with, each A person across the whole group will be playing the role of a supervisor, each B person will be playing the role of a supervisee and each C person will be playing the role of an observer. If the numbers within the group do not divide exactly by three, and you have one or more groups of four, then clearly some people will need to be allocated the letter D, and they will be additional observers.

▶ Distribute copies of **Worksheet 3: Giving feedback** to each participant. Here they will see mini-scenarios. Explain to the group that, to begin with, they will be using Scenario 1. Allow a few minutes for person A to give feedback to person B relating to this scenario while person C (and possibly person D) observes. Begin the role play.

▶ After three or four minutes, indicate to the group that the first stage of the role play is now over. Give them a few minutes to debrief; that is, allow the supervisor and supervisee to comment on how they feel the process worked out, and give the observers the opportunity to make any comments they feel are relevant. Overall, this should take approximately 10 minutes from the beginning of the role play to the end of the feedback; this is quite a tight timescale and so it will be necessary to police this part of the exercise quite closely.

▶ Next, repeat the exercise, moving people's roles along one position – that is, B should now be the person giving the feedback, C should be the person receiving the feedback, and A (and possibly D) should observe. This time they should use the second scenario on the worksheet.

▶ They should follow a similar process, again within a 10 minute timescale, of a few minutes of brief feedback, followed by debriefing and discussion of what can be learned from seeing that feedback in action.

▶ Next, conclude by allowing the exercise to be run a third time, again with people switching roles along the alphabet. This time they should use Scenario 3 from the worksheet. This overall process should take 30 minutes, or no longer than 35, if at all possible. Once this round of role plays and debriefing has been completed, reconvene the main group to focus on the main lessons to be learned from having practised these skills.

▶ Please note that this is quite a full and demanding exercise. It is likely that a lot of issues will arise. If you wish, you may find it helpful to focus simply on the main points in this exercise and postpone more detailed discussion for a further exercise or session within the same course.

▶ Use the last few minutes to summarise the key points to have emerged from the discussion, recording these on the flip chart sheet. Take the opportunity to emphasise that giving feedback skilfully is an important part of making supervision *reflective* supervision.

Worksheet 3: Giving feedback

Scenario 1

Chris has been late every morning this week and was also late a couple of times last week. You are not aware of any reason, such as transport difficulties, why this might be the case. Other members of staff who get to work on time are clearly becoming resentful of what they regard as Chris's lack of commitment.

Scenario 2

Kim's overall standard of work is very good, but her written work is the exception. It is often of poor quality (lacking clarity, repetitive, ungrammatical, containing a lot of irrelevant material) and there appears to be no sign of it improving, despite the fact that you have already pointed out these problems previously.

Scenario 3

Pat seems to get on well with most people, although there does seem to be a problem in terms of attitudes towards some staff, in particular Kim. Pat seems to find fault with anything Kim does and is sometimes less than polite in dealing with Kim. Things are going to get out of hand if something is not done soon.

Exercise 6: Helping people learn

Aim

This is a group discussion exercise.

Materials

Flip chart paper and pens or white board and pens

Slide 3: The Kolb learning cycle

Timing

This exercise will need 60 to 80 minutes.

Introduction: 5 minutes

Presentation of the Kolb learning cycle: 10 minutes

Small group exercise: 25 minutes

Feedback and discussion: 30 minutes

Summary and conclusion: 5 minutes

Activity

▶ Begin by explaining to the group that this exercise focuses on how people learn, and therefore how they can be helped to learn through supervision. Using **Slide 3: The Kolb learning cycle**, present to the group the main points relating to the Kolb learning cycle. Give a brief example of each of the four stages as illustrated on the slide. Allow time for questions and discussion before dividing the main group into subgroups of four to six participants.

▶ Once the participants are in their subgroups, give them the task of exploring how they would help someone to learn using the Kolb learning cycle. It is helpful to point out to participants at this stage that they may find it a useful way forward to consider what obstacles may arise in terms of people's learning. These obstacles can be related systematically to each of the four stages of the Kolb learning cycle.

▶ Once the groups have had enough time to explore the issues in some detail, reconvene the main group and use this as an opportunity for a plenary feedback discussion session. This should allow plenty of time to bring out the main learning points. One thing that should emerge clearly is that different people learn in different ways and may therefore get stuck at different points in the learning cycle.

▶ Use the last few minutes of the exercise to sum up the key points to have emerged, or ask the group to do so.

Exercise 7: Hopes and fears

Aim

In this session the participants will be able to air their hopes and fears about their role as a supervisor. This can be a very helpful exercise to enable people to see what they have in common with other supervisors and what their own personal issues are.

Materials

Flip chart paper and pens or white board and pens

Worksheet 4: Hopes and fears (for version 2 only)

Timing

There are two versions of this exercise, short and long. The short version can be completed in 30 to 40 minutes, while the longer version is likely to take 60 to 80 minutes.

Activity

▶ *Version 1:* This is a short(ish), snappy exercise that can be used early on in a course or programme of study. It involves asking the group to work in pairs or trios to identify their hopes and fears in relation to their role as supervisors. After 10 to 15 minutes reconvene the main group and begin a plenary feedback session. Make it clear that it is acceptable to keep certain things confidential, but it would be helpful if they could be as candid as they reasonably can be, as this will help everyone to learn more from the exercise.

▶ During the feedback and discussion, help the group to identify common themes that emerge and record these on the whiteboard or flip chart. Conclude by summing up the key learning points or ask the group to do so. As part of this make the point that many of the fears are very common and understandable, so there is scope for people helping each other to deal with these, while some issues are personal to the individual concerned, and so he or she should consider raising these concerns in their own supervision with their line manager or with any other trusted mentor.

▶ *Version 2:* This is a fuller exercise that can be used early on in a course or programme of study or towards the end. Begin by explaining that the object of the exercise is to explore hopes and fears to see which ones are shared views and which ones relate to specific individuals and their own circumstances. Give each participant a copy of **Worksheet 4: Hopes and fears**. Next, ask the group to work in pairs or trios to identify their hopes and fears in relation to their role as supervisors. Invite them to use the first page of the worksheet to record these.

▶ Reassure the group that these worksheets will remain confidential and that you will not be collecting them in or asking group members to show them to other people.

▶ After 10 to 20 minutes (depending on how much time you have available) reconvene the main group and begin a plenary feedback session. As with Version 1, make it clear that it is acceptable to keep certain things confidential, but it would be helpful if they could be as candid as they reasonably can, as this will help everyone to learn more from the exercise.

▶ During the feedback and discussion help the group to identify common themes that emerge and record these on the white board or flip chart. Begin to bring the session to a close by summing up the key learning points, or ask the group to do so. As part of this, make the point that many of the fears are very common and understandable, so there is scope for people helping each other to deal with these, while some issues are personal to the individual concerned, and so he or she should consider raising these concerns in their own supervision with their line manager or with any other trusted mentor.

▶ Finally, point out to the group that the second page of the worksheet gives them some homework to do. Explain that they are likely to find it helpful to complete this part of the worksheet at the earliest opportunity after the course (either alone or jointly with their line manager or mentor), as this will facilitate addressing both the common issues and the more individualised ones.

Worksheet 4: Hopes and fears (part 1)

What hopes and fears do you have about your role as a supervisor?

Hopes

Fears

Worksheet 4: Hopes and fears (part 2)

To be completed later: What do you need to do in the coming weeks and months in order to make your hopes as achievable as possible and to address your concerns and fears as fully as you can? Who can support you in this?

Exercise 8: Giving support

Aim

This activity involves brainstorming and exploring various forms of support.

Materials

Flip chart paper and pens or white board and pens

Timing

This exercise should take between 40 and 60 minutes, but may be extended if so wished.

Activity

▶ Begin the exercise by explaining to the group that an important part of the supervisory role is helping staff to feel that they are fully supported in the difficult tasks that they undertake. Make it clear to participants that this exercise will concentrate on the wide variety of ways of supporting people.

▶ Next, ask the group to break into pairs and to share with one another examples of when they have felt most supported by their line manager in the recent or distant past. Explain to the group that these discussions are confidential; that is, they will not be asked to feed back any personal or confidential matters to the group. Allow five to ten minutes for this work in pairs.

▶ Once the work in pairs has been concluded, reconvene the main group and take feedback from them concerning the range of issues that have arisen. Emphasise that it is not necessary for people to betray confidences or to name names, and that what is required for the discussion to be a success is for people to give general examples of what steps and/or processes they have found helpful and supportive in the past. Allow approximately 20 minutes for this part of the exercise.

▶ Once you have concluded this section use the flip chart or white board as a basis for a brainstorming session. Ask the participants to identify as many sources of support as they can. Make it clear to the group that you are looking at both forms of support – support systems within the organisation, such as training and development, grievance procedures and so on, as well as informal sources of support such as camaraderie among colleagues, support from friends and neighbours and so on. Do not discuss these issues as they are mentioned; simply record them so that you can get as many as possible onto the board within the time available.

▶ Once you are satisfied that the group has come up with a sufficiently extensive list (without labouring the exercise), stop the brainstorming session and then invite comments about the exercise. This should enable participants to identify patterns and issues arising from the wide array of support mechanisms identified and recorded on the board.

▶ From this, it should be possible to deduce a number of principles for giving support. That is, the work done in pairs to identify what individuals have found particularly supportive will give some indication of the depth of support that can be made available, while the brainstorming exercise will focus on the breadth of support that can, in principle at least, be available to staff. The concluding discussion helps to pull together both breadth and depth by trying to identify as explicitly as possible a number of principles for effectively supporting staff. These principles should be recorded on a sheet of flip chart paper so that they can be typed up at a later date and distributed to participants, as this list can be an invaluable source of guidance for future supervisory practice.

▶ Use the last few minutes to sum up the main learning points of the exercise, or ask the group to do so.

Exercise 9: Mediation

Aim

This is an exercise based on problem-solving and dispute resolution techniques.

Materials

Flip chart paper and pens or white board and pens

Sheets of A4 paper

Slide 4: Mediation

Timing

This exercise should take at least 60 minutes, and possibly as much as 80.

Activity

▶ Using **Slide 4: Mediation**, explain to the group the role and purpose of mediation within the context of supervisory management. Make it clear to the participants that a line manager is neither exclusively the 'champion' of his or her staff, nor a source of pressure from above for those staff.

▶ Rather, he or she acts as a cog in the wheel of the organisation linking the two layers of staff and higher management. Allow time for questions and discussion about this issue, as it is likely that some participants may take a different view regarding the line manager's role as a leader of his or her staff group and therefore not being in an intermediary position. It may be necessary to point out carefully, sensitively and constructively that this is not the case within modern organisations and is out of step with supervisory management practice.

▶ Once there has been sufficient discussion about these issues and you are ready to proceed, move on to the next stage in the exercise. This involves asking each participant to use a single sheet of A4 paper to record brief details of an example of tension between the staff they supervise and the higher management to whom they are answerable as a line manager. You may need to give some examples of this from your own experience to get them going, that is, to give them a clear picture of what you are expecting from them.

▶ Once they have written down the brief details, ask them to fold the sheet over once and then a second time so that it is now a quarter of its original size. Collect these from each of the group members, shuffle them and then hand them out again to the group participants, so that each person should again have a single sheet, but not their own. By sheer coincidence it may work out that somebody actually does receive his or her own sheet back. If this occurs simply arrange a 'swap' with somebody else at random in the group once it emerges that this is the case. This should not present a problem.

▶ Next, ask the group to divide into pairs or threes and to open their sheets and share the information on the sheets. Explain to them that their task is to explore together how they feel they could tackle the tension identified on the sheet of paper they have been given. Make it clear that what you are looking for is not a clear, precise step-by-step action plan for dealing with the issue, as they will not have enough information available to them to come up with a realistic plan of that type. Instead, what is required of them is a general analysis of what sort of actions can be taken in order to help resolve disputes and conflicts of interest between staff who are supervised and the wider management hierarchy. This should produce extensive discussion.

▶ Once you feel that you have spent enough time working in the small groups, reconvene the main group and use the material generated in the pairs and trios to form the basis of a broader discussion about the principles of good practice relating to conflict resolution. The focus of this discussion should be what steps supervisors can take in order to act as mediators between the interest of the staff they supervise and the wider organisation they represent.

▶ Once again, leave the last few minutes to sum up the main learning points arising from the discussions, or ask the group to do so.

Exercise 10: Problems in supervision

Aim

This is an exercise which involves exploring the various problems which are likely to arise at one time or another within the supervisory process.

Timing

This exercise should take between 60 and 80 minutes.

Materials

Flip chart paper and pens or white board and pens

Activity

▶ This exercise should begin with a brief introduction that explains to the participants that problems in supervision are likely to occur in a variety of forms. It should be emphasised that encountering problems in supervision is not necessarily the sign of a bad supervisor. Rather, it is a reflection of the complexity and difficulty of the supervisory task.

▶ The next stage in the exercise is a brainstorming activity. This involves inviting group members to identify actual or potential problems in supervision. These should be recorded on the flip chart or on the white board so that they are visible to the whole group. Try to encourage participants to be as forthcoming as possible; again, emphasise that problems cannot be equated with weakness or poor quality of supervision. It should also be emphasised that they need not have experienced the problems they are indicating, but merely that they are aware of them, so that the list on the board can be as full as possible. This should take 5 to 10 minutes, allowing for brief discussion of items as they arise, but not going into great detail about such matters.

▶ Once you have completed the list on the board or are satisfied that you have enough items to work with, invite the group to identify any possible patterns that may occur – for example, problems around clarity of focus, problems around interpersonal perceptions and so on. If such patterns can be easily discerned, these can be used as a basis of structuring the next stage of the exercise. If no such patterns can be discerned, then the next stage of the exercise should be structured along fairly random lines.

▶ The next part of the process involves dividing the main group into subgroups of four to six people. Once the groups are assembled, allocate to them a number of identified problems from the main list. As stated earlier, if there is a clear pattern of problems, then use this as the basis for allocating the problems logically to the groups. Once the groups have been allocated the list of problems, ask them to come up with a range of possible solutions to such problems. Each subgroup should be issued with a sheet of flip chart paper and a pen to enable them to record the main points of their discussion. It is important to explain to the group that you are not looking for 'magic answers', and that this is simply an opportunity to explore possible strategies for tackling some of the many problems that are likely to arise in supervision over time. Allow approximately 25 minutes for this part of the process.

▶ Once the groups have had adequate opportunity to explore the issues and record their points, reconvene the main group and chair a plenary feedback and discussion session in which the opportunity should be taken to draw out themes and issues, rather than simply repeating in the main group discussions that have arisen in the small groups.

▶ Use the last few minutes of the session to sum up the main points that have arisen, or ask the group to do so.

Exercise 11: Destructive processes in supervision

Aim

This is an exercise that will allow participants to explore a range of processes which can have a destructive effect for both supervisor and supervisee.

Timing

It is recommended that 80 minutes be allocated for this exercise.

Materials

Flip chart paper and pens or white board and pens

Slide 5: Destructive processes in supervision

Worksheet 5: Destructive processes in supervision

Activity

▶ Explain to the group that the focus of this exercise is the range of destructive processes that can occur in supervision. As with Exercise 10, emphasise that the existence of a destructive process is not necessarily a sign of a poor or inadequate supervisor, but rather a reflection of the complexities of interpersonal relationships. Point out to the group that destructive processes are very common in human relationships in general and that supervision is no exception to this.

▶ Next, using **Slide 5: Destructive processes in supervision**, go through the list of identified destructive processes, explaining each one briefly and, where possible, giving an example. Invite questions and discussion throughout the presentation so that this is not a simple list of processes, but rather an opportunity to discuss them and their significance.

▶ The overall process should therefore take about 30 minutes. Once this part of the exercise is complete, distribute copies of **Worksheet 5: Destructive processes in supervision** to the participants and ask them to work in pairs or threes to answer the questions on the sheet. This should take 20 to 25 minutes, thus allowing time for plenary feedback and discussion to compare notes relating to the range of issues that are likely to have occurred. This should be a good opportunity to emphasise the dangers of destructive processes and how relatively common they are. Participants can be helped to look at ways in which they can identify such destructive processes and develop steps to prevent or stop these processes once they have begun.

▶ Use the last few minutes to sum up the key points, or ask the group to do so.

Worksheet 5: Destructive processes in supervision

1. How might you recognise one or more destructive processes?

2. How might you respond once you become aware of the operation of one or more destructive processes?

3. What steps could you take to prevent destructive processes from occurring?

Exercise 12: Quotes

Aim

This activity gives participants the opportunity to explore varying views about supervision, to allow them to deepen and broaden their understanding of what is involved.

Timing

Allow about 80 minutes for this exercise.

Materials

Flip chart paper and pens or white board and pens

Worksheet 6: Quotes

Activity

▶ Begin by explaining to the group that this exercise will involve looking at comments about supervision as a basis for discussing some of the complexities involved. Explain that it will not be a matter of trying to come up with 'the right answer', but rather of using the comments as a means of developing a helpful discussion. Next divide the group into subgroups of four to six people and give each participant a copy of **Worksheet 6: Quotes**. Invite them to work together in their groups to answer the questions on the worksheet.

▶ After about 30 to 35 minutes, ask the group to stop working on the questions and to spend the next 5 to 10 minutes trying to draw out the lessons they feel can be learned by discussing the comments and the conclusions that can be drawn. After this period reconvene the main group and begin a plenary feedback and discussion session. Try to make sure that the discussion focuses on the lessons to be learned, rather than allowing it to get bogged down in the minutiae of the specific comments or their reactions to them (but do allow some scope for people airing their views about specifics).

▶ Use the last 5 to 10 minutes to help the group to identify a minimum of five key learning points to emerge from the exercise. Record these on the flip chart or white board. If possible, try to aim for 10, but don't push this too hard if the group shows any signs of struggling with this. It is important not to end on a negative note.

Worksheet 6: Quotes

For each of the following comments, please consider:

1. Why do you think the person concerned may have said this?

2. What concerns does the comment raise for you?

3. How might you want to respond to this situation?

Supervision is just a way for managers to check up on us. It's oppressive.

I dread supervision; it's just a talking shop. Nothing seems to change.

I don't trust my supervisor. I think s/he's got a hidden agenda.

My supervisor and I have become really good friends. It's great.

Supervision doesn't work for me. We just don't get on – I think it's a personality clash.

I never learn anything from supervision. We just go through my cases and I am no better off at the end than I was at the beginning.

My supervisor seems more interested in counselling me than helping me improve my work. What's that all about?

My supervisor takes no interest in me as a person. I am just a work machine to him/her.

Supervision keeps getting cancelled. My supervisor seems to be too busy to fit it in.

We are always late starting supervision. My supervisor always has things s/he needs to sort out before we can start.

Exercise 13: The balance of support and challenge

Aim

This is an exercise that explores the relationship between supporting supervisees and providing a challenge for them.

Timing

This is a relatively short exercise and can normally be completed within 30 to 40 minutes.

Materials

Flip chart paper and pens or whiteboard and pens

Slide 6: Balance of support and challenge

Activity

▶ Explain to the group that this exercise involves exploring how supervision can be both supportive and challenging, and that the balance of these two characteristics can be very effective.

▶ Next, show the group **Slide 6: Balance of support and challenge**, indicating how the diagram works in terms of the two axes of support (down) and challenge (across). Briefly explain what the diagram represents in terms of the four squares created by the intersection of the two axes.

▶ Next, draw on the flip chart sheet a line down and a line across to imitate the slide. Ask the group to say how they would feel if they were to be supervised according to each of the four squares; that is, ask for comments about how they would feel if they had a supervisor who was high in support but low in challenge, for example. Record their comments in the appropriate square on the flip chart sheet. Repeat this pattern until you have completed the full diagram with all four squares. This exercise works best if you start with the square in the top right-hand corner, then proceed to the bottom right-hand corner, then move across to the bottom left, and conclude with the top left-hand corner.

▶ What should emerge from this process is that the first three squares produce generally very negative and unhelpful consequences, while the fourth square – that is, the combination of high support and high challenge – produces very positive outcomes in which supervisees feel both valued and supported on the one hand, but also reassured and secure that they are being monitored and helped through the discipline of being challenged appropriately and constructively by their line manager on the other. Once this process has been completed there will be time for you to have a discussion about the implications of this. If you wish to pursue this in more detail you will be able to do so, but you may simply wish to have a brief concluding discussion. As usual, you should end by summarising the main points that have arisen or asking the group to do so.

Exercise 14: Good management vs bullying

Aim

This exercise involves comparing a list of characteristics of good managers with a list of characteristics of bullying managers. The aim of the session is to explore the main differences between the two lists.

Timing

It is envisaged that 80 minutes will be required for this exercise.

Materials

Flip chart paper and pens

Slide 7: Good management vs bullying (1)

Slide 8: Good management vs bullying (2)

Activity

▶ It is important to be clear at the beginning of this exercise that there are significant differences between good management practices in supervision and what is often referred to these days as bullying or harassment. Explain to the group that the object of the exercise is to establish which aspects of good management practice differ from aspects of bullying and harassment.

▶ Next, using **Slides 7 and 8: Good management vs bullying**, show the group the range of characteristics which can be used to describe a good manager. Contrast these with the column on the right which list the equivalent for a bullying boss. It is unlikely that there will be any major disagreements with what is listed on the slide, but you may wish to leave a small amount of time for discussion of any of these issues in case there is a difference of opinion.

▶ Once you have presented this list to the group, divide them up into subgroups of four to six participants. Issue each group with a sheet of flip chart paper and a pen, and ask them to record their views about:

  ▶ how they would know whether any items from the second list (that is, the bullying list) are present in their own practice

  ▶ what steps can be taken to ensure that the characteristics on the good management list are maximised and those on the bullying list are not allowed to predominate.

▶ Allow 25 to 30 minutes for this discussion to take place in small groups. Once this time has elapsed, ask the group to display their sheets of flip chart paper on the walls (if allowed by the owners of the venue) and allow a few minutes for participants to wander around the room looking at the range of points that the other groups have come up with, comparing and contrasting their own group's work.

▶ Once you have allowed a few minutes for this, reconvene the main group and begin a plenary feedback and discussion session to draw out the learning points from the exercise. This should enable the group to appreciate the significant differences between good management and bullying, and thereby challenge the myth that bullying is simply a form of strong leadership. Finally, sum up the main points to have arisen from the exercise, or ask the group to do so.

Exercise 15: The four elements of supervision

Aim

This exercise enables participants to appreciate the breadth of the supervisory role.

Timing

This exercise should take approximately 60 minutes, although you may wish to extend it if you feel there is a need to do so.

Materials

Flip chart paper and pens or white board and pens

Slide 9: The four elements of supervision

Activity

▶ It is important to begin this exercise by emphasising to the group that supervision is a broad activity and is not simply a matter of ensuring that staff have undertaken their duties. This aspect of accountability or standard setting is an important part of the role. However, this exercise will help participants to understand that supervision is much broader than a narrow focus on accountability.

▶ Using **Slide 9: The four elements of supervision**, explain to the group the four different elements of supervision: accountability, staff development, staff care and mediation. Give a brief explanation of each of these four terms, ideally giving at least one example of each. Allow opportunities for discussion to develop at this stage. Once you have completed this part of the exercise you can then invite comments, questions and general discussion around these issues from the group. It is our experience that this generates a number of questions and points from participants. This discussion can be very useful to get across a number of points about good practice in supervisory management. It is also useful as a forum for allowing participants to raise any issues which have not come up under any of the other exercises as part of the course or staff development exercise you are running.

▶ Use the last few minutes to summarise the main points to have emerged, or ask the group to do so.

Exercise 16: Recording supervision

Aim

This activity helps to establish what is good (and not so good) practice in keeping a record of supervision.

Timing

Allow 60 to 80 minutes.

Materials

Flip chart paper and pens or white board and pens

Handout 1: Recording supervision

Worksheet 7: Recording supervision

Activity

▶ Begin by explaining to the group that this activity will help them to learn about recording supervision sessions and avoiding some of the related pitfalls. Next, divide the main group into subgroups of four to six people and give each participant a copy of **Handout 1: Recording supervision** and **Worksheet 7: Recording supervision**. Once they are settled, invite them to read over the handout (which contains excerpts from supervision records). When they have done this, invite them to help each other to complete the worksheet, which asks them questions about the excerpts. Please note that this exercise may need some close supervision, as some people may not appreciate the significance of some of the issues involved in the excerpts – the 'presenter' version of the handout should be useful to help you nudge them in the right direction.

▶ After 20 to 25 minutes reconvene the main group and begin a plenary feedback and discussion session. You may find the 'presenter' copy of the handout helpful for guiding the discussion to make sure the greatest possible number of important points come out.

▶ Use the last 5 to 10 minutes of the session to go round the room asking each participant to name one thing they will do differently in recording supervision or one important point they will bear in mind.

Handout 1: Recording supervision

Excerpts from supervision records

'Excerpt 1: Pam is having marital difficulties at the moment, so we discussed what extra support she will need at this difficult time.

Excerpt 2: Jack wanted to talk about his professional development, so I agreed to look out for suitable courses for him.

Excerpt 3: Anne's work in this area is very weak. I made it clear to her that she must improve.

Excerpt 4: Kira talked about feeling racially harassed by Joan and Ellen. I told her that she needs to be less sensitive about such matters and to learn how to get on better with people. She needs to understand that she will make herself unpopular if she goes around making allegations.

Excerpt 5: Paul described the difficulties he had had at the planning meeting. He told me how several people did not get involved and how frustrated he felt by this. I told him I could fully understand how he felt. He went on to say that the situation had left him feeling uneasy about other meetings. I asked him what he might do about this, but he was unsure what he could do. I suggested he might want to talk to Sarah about it as she used to chair those meetings and she had never had these problems. Paul said he would do that but would find it difficult to fit it into his busy schedule. I explained that it was important for him to make the time as the problem wasn't simply going to go away. He then said that ...

Excerpt 6: Very useful supervision session again. Nothing specific to report.

Excerpt 7: Ravi is new to working in the child protection field. He is doing well so far and is beginning to understand that child abuse is not acceptable in our culture.

Excerpt 8: We discussed Sam's workload. She claimed that she was overloaded but I told her that it is the same for everybody in the team.

Excerpt 9: I have been worried about my role as convenor of the supervision development group, so we spent a lot of the session looking at how I could deal with some of the difficulties involved. Ian was very helpful in suggesting ways forward.

Excerpt 10: Everyone in the team is concerned about the new hot-desking arrangements, so much of the supervision session was spent discussing how the team can deal with the issues involved.'

Handout 1: Recording supervision (Presenter's version)

Excerpts from supervision records

Excerpt 1: Pam is having marital difficulties at the moment, so we discussed what extra support she will need at this difficult time.

This raises issues of confidentiality. It would have been better to record something like 'having personal difficulties of a confidential nature'.

Excerpt 2: Jack wanted to talk about his professional development, so I agreed to look out for suitable courses for him.

For one thing, there is more to professional development than looking out for suitable courses. A good supervisor should be helping supervisees to draw out the learning from their experience, supporting them in developing reflective practice. Training should be seen as the icing on the cake when it comes to learning – most of the learning should arise from practice itself (facilitated by skilful supervision). For another thing, it is not helpful for the supervisor to take responsibility for finding suitable courses. It would be more appropriate for him or her to encourage the supervisee to do their own research into what opportunities are available, to encourage them to take responsibility for their own learning.

Excerpt 3: Anne's work in this area is very weak. I made it clear to her that she must improve.

Even if Anne's work is weak, this could have been worded more tactfully and supportively. As it stands, it sounds like a negative and judgemental comment, rather than a helpful piece of constructive feedback. Is all of Anne's work 'weak'? Or are there areas of strength to counterbalance some of the areas for development? If so, it would be helpful to mention these too, to give a more balanced picture.

Excerpt 4: Kira talked about feeling racially harassed by Joan and Ellen. I told her that she needs to be less sensitive about such matters and to learn how to get on better with people. She needs to understand that she will make herself unpopular if she goes around making allegations.

It perhaps goes without saying that it is unacceptable to think this, let alone record it. There is, of course, a moral and professional obligation to take any such concerns seriously and investigate them in line with the appropriate policy within the organisation concerned.

Excerpt 5: Paul described the difficulties he had had at the planning meeting. He told me how several people did not get involved and how frustrated he felt by this. I told him I could fully understand how he felt. He went on to say that the situation had left him feeling uneasy about other meetings. I asked him what he might do about this, but he was unsure what he could do. I suggested he might want to talk to Sarah about it as she used to chair those meetings and she never had these problems. Paul said he would do that but would find it difficult to fit it into his busy schedule. I explained that it was important for him to make the time as the problem wasn't simply going to go away. He then said that ...

There is no need to record this amount of detail. It is a waste of valuable time and serves no useful purpose. This could lead to a very useful discussion about how to decide what to record and what to leave out, what is relevant and what is not.

Excerpt 6: Very useful supervision session again. Nothing specific to report.

This, of course, goes to the opposite extreme and is far too vague. This point can feed the discussion about getting the balance right – recording what needs to be recorded, nothing more, nothing less.

Excerpt 7: Ravi is new to working in the child protection field. He is doing well so far and is beginning to understand that child abuse is not acceptable in our culture.

This seems to assume that child abuse is acceptable in Ravi's culture and is therefore potentially a racist comment. This could lead to a useful discussion about how issues relating to challenging racism can be handled in supervision.

Excerpt 8: We discussed Sam's workload. She claimed that she was overloaded but I told her that it is the same for everybody in the team.

If it is indeed the case that everyone in the team is overloaded, then this should clearly be a matter of concern for the supervisor, as it is identifying a staff care need. If it is not the case that it is 'the same for everybody', then the supervisor is fobbing this supervisee off. So, either way, this is not a wise response to a concern being raised about work overload.

Excerpt 9: I have been worried about my role as convenor of the supervision development group, so we spent a lot of the session looking at how I could deal with some of the difficulties involved. Ian was very helpful in suggesting ways forward.

This raises the question: whose supervision session is this? This sort of problem is particularly common in situations where the supervisor has a poor or non-existent relationship with their own supervisor and is therefore reduced to seeking help about their own issues inappropriately from their supervisees. This is not to say that supervisors cannot ask colleagues for advice or feedback about issues, but it should not be done in a supervision session where the focus should be on the supervisee's needs and not the supervisor's.

Excerpt 10: Everyone in the team is concerned about the new hot-desking arrangements so much of the supervision session was spent discussing how the team can deal with the issues involved.

If this is an issue that affects the whole team, why is it being dealt with in an individual supervision session rather than at a team meeting? This is a common mistake among inexperienced or unconfident supervisors who feel more comfortable discussing issues on a one-to-one basis than with the whole group. This is potentially very problematic because: (i) it is wasteful of time, as the same discussion will be repeated unnecessarily in several supervision sessions; (ii) each supervisee's valuable one-to-one supervision time will be taken up by wider team issues; and (iii) the team will not have the opportunity to discuss collectively an issue or set of issues that affects the team collectively.

Worksheet 7: Recording supervision

For each of the 10 excerpts on the handout, consider whether you feel this is an appropriate comment to make. If you feel it is not, please record why you think it is not, and what issues it raises.

Excerpt 1:

Excerpt 2:

Excerpt 3:

Excerpt 4:

Excerpt 5:

Excerpt 6:

Excerpt 7:

Excerpt 8:

Excerpt 9:

Excerpt 10:

Exercise 17: Managing poor performance

Aim

This is a case study exercise designed to help participants tackle what is often seen as a very challenging aspect of supervision, namely, managing poor performance in individual supervisees.

Timing

This activity will take a minimum of 60 minutes; preferably, 80 minutes should be allocated.

Materials

Flip chart paper and pens or white board and pens

Worksheet 8: Managing poor performance

Activity

▶ Begin by explaining to the group that the focus of this exercise is the challenge presented by poor performance. It will be helpful to comment that it is generally recognised that managing poor performance is an aspect of supervision that few people relish. However, there are positive steps that can be taken to make sure that managing poor performance is a constructive and helpful part of supervision. It need not be a distressing or unhelpful process. Explain to the group that the basis of the exercise will be an analysis of case material.

▶ Next, divide the main group into four subgroups. Distribute copies of **Worksheet 8: Managing poor performance**, which presents the four scenarios. Allocate one scenario to each of the four groups and give them the task of developing an action plan for:

  ▶ what issues they would take into consideration in addressing the situation described

  ▶ what actual steps they would take

▶ Allow 25 to 30 minutes for this stage of the exercise. Once this part has been completed, reconvene the main group and then chair a plenary feedback and discussion session to allow each of the groups to make a short presentation about the issues arising from their case study and the steps that they would take.

▶ Once each group has had the opportunity to feed back the findings from their examination of their case study, invite the whole group to draw out from the discussions the principles of good practice for managing poor performance. Use the flip chart to record a number of conclusions that can be drawn about how best to manage poor performance.

▶ Use the last few minutes of the session to draw out the key points, or ask the group to do so.

NB This exercise uses the same scenarios as the Giving Feedback exercise, with a further one added. It could therefore be used as a replacement for the Giving Feedback exercise or as a follow-up to it. If the latter, try to make sure that the group builds on the earlier work, rather than simply repeats it.

Worksheet 8: Managing poor performance

Scenario 1

Chris has been late every morning this week and was also late a couple of times last week. You are not aware of any reason, such as transport difficulties, why this might be the case. Other members of staff who get to work on time are clearly becoming resentful of what they regard as Chris's lack of commitment.

Scenario 2

Kim's overall standard of work is very good, but her written work is the exception. It is often of poor quality (lacking clarity, repetitive, ungrammatical, containing a lot of irrelevant material) and there appears to be no sign of it improving, despite the fact that you have already pointed out these problems previously.

Scenario 3

Pat seems to get on well with most people, although there does seem to be a problem in terms of attitudes towards some staff, in particular Kim. Pat seems to find fault with anything Kim does and is sometimes less than polite in dealing with Kim. Things are going to get out of hand if something is not done soon.

Scenario 4

Bernie promised to make a number of enquiries and to feed back to the next team meeting. Everyone was very disappointed when the next meeting began and it very quickly became clear that Bernie had not done what had been promised. After the meeting, Bernie's colleagues complain to you that this is not the first time they have been let down in this way.

Exercise 18: Promoting anti-discriminatory practice

Aim

In this exercise participants will be able to learn about tools they can use to promote anti-discriminatory practice, and thereby promote equality and value diversity.

Timing

60 to 80 minutes.

Materials

Flip chart, paper and pens or white board and pens

Worksheet 9: Promoting anti-discriminatory practice

Slide 10: Tools for promoting anti-discriminatory practice

Activity

▶ Begin by explaining to the group that the focus of this session will be on helping them to make sure that their supervisees are working in ways that are consistent with anti-discriminatory practice. Next, using **Slide 10: Tools for promoting anti-discriminatory practice**, give a short presentation on 'Tools for promoting equality'. Allow 15 to 20 minutes for the presentation and a further 15 to 20 for discussion (whether you take questions during the presentation or ask people to wait until the end is up to you – the former is likely to generate more discussion, but either way can work well). Use **Worksheet 9: Promoting anti-discriminatory practice** to inform your presentation, but do make sure that you don't simply read out the worksheet; participants will need a fuller understanding than the worksheet gives them.

▶ After the presentation and discussion invite the participants to work in pairs or threes. Give each participant a copy of the worksheet and explain to them that their task is to work together to answer the questions on the sheet. Allow 15 to 20 minutes for this part of the exercise (depending on how long the presentation and discussion have taken and how long you have allocated to the overall exercise).

▶ When you are ready, reconvene the main group and begin a plenary feedback and discussion session. During the discussion, record key learning points on the flip chart or white board.

▶ Use the last few minutes to sum up the learning from the session or ask the group to do so.

Worksheet 9: Promoting anti-discriminatory practice

For each of the tools, please consider: (i) whether it is applicable in your work setting; (ii) if it is, how might you use it to best effect? If it is not suitable for your setting, could you adapt it or is there an alternative way of addressing the same issues?

Why? Asking a supervisee why they did something in particular way will help to 'surface' their values. This can then lead to a discussion of their values as they relate to ensuring fairness and equality.

What if? This is the 'hypothetical approach' and involves reversing key elements of a situation to see what difference it makes: What if this white person were black? What if this woman were a man? What if this 82-year-old were 42 years old? In each case, what difference would it make?

Power analysis: This involves asking the supervisee to identify who has what power in a situation. Who has power over what (or whom)? In what circumstances? When and how might the balance of power change? This helps to show the complexities of power (and power as the basis of discrimination).

PCS analysis: Based on Neil Thompson's work in this area, this involves looking at situations and the potential for discrimination within them in terms of the three levels: Personal (possible prejudices and unfair attitudes towards certain groups of people), Cultural (taken for granted assumptions, stereotypes and so on) and Structural (inequalities based on the structure of society in terms of class, race, gender and so on).

SWOT analysis: By analysing situations in terms of the (present) strengths and weaknesses and (future) opportunities and threats, we can develop a picture that is helpful for considering how equality issues fit into that picture and how they can be incorporated into the way the situation is understood.

Demographic analysis: This can be a useful exercise for supervisees new to the area. Set them the task of finding out key demographic indicators as they relate to possible discrimination: ethnic breakdown of local population; number and range of languages spoken; numbers of people living below the poverty line; proportion of disabled people in the area; percentage of people above retirement age and so on.

Exercise 19: Developing reflective practice

Aim

This activity is designed to help participants appreciate the value and importance of reflective practice.

Timing

This activity should take about 60 minutes in total.

Materials

Flip chart paper and pens or white board and pens

Worksheet 10: Developing reflective practice

Activity

▶ Begin by explaining to the group that this exercise is geared towards recognising the importance of developing reflecting practice.

▶ Divide the main group into subgroups of four to six participants and give each one a copy of **Worksheet 10: Developing reflective practice**. Ask the groups to work together to complete the worksheet. Allow about 20 minutes for this.

▶ Next, reconvene the main group and begin a process of taking feedback, using this as an opportunity to draw out some important points about the value of reflective practice.

▶ Use the last few minutes to sum up the learning from the session, or ask the group to do so.

Worksheet 10: Developing reflective practice

Work with your colleagues in the group to answer the following two questions:

1. What are the benefits of using reflective practice as a foundation for your work?

2. What are the dangers of adopting a non-reflective approach – that is, an unthinking approach based on habit, routine, guesswork or just copying others?

Exercise 20: Avoiding the drama triangle

Aim

This activity helps participants to understand the importance of avoiding the development of a destructive three-way relationship.

Materials

Flip chart paper and pens or whiteboard and pens

Handout 2: Avoiding the drama triangle

Worksheet 11: Avoiding the drama triangle

Timing

60 to 80 minutes.

Activity

▶ Begin by explaining that this session will focus on what is known as 'the drama triangle' and will explain why it is important to avoid its clutches. Next, give every participant a copy of **Handout 2: Avoiding the drama triangle**. Spend 5 or 10 minutes going through the handout and giving participants the opportunity to ask questions and confirm their understanding.

▶ Following this, divide the group into subgroups of four to six people and give each participant a copy of **Worksheet 11: Avoiding the drama triangle**. Explain that their task is to help one another to answer the questions on the worksheet.

▶ After 20 to 25 minutes, reconvene the main group and begin a plenary feedback and discussion session. If the point does not emerge spontaneously from the discussion, make sure that the group are aware of just how common the drama triangle is in life in general and in supervision settings in particular. Make sure it is clear, too, just how destructive it can be.

▶ Use the last few minutes to sum up the learning, or invite the group to do so.

Handout 2: Avoiding the drama triangle

The drama triangle

'The helping professions tend to attract people who want to make a difference to other people's lives, but this enthusiasm for offering support and trying to "make things better" can become problematic if care is not taken to maintain appropriate boundaries when involved in situations of conflict. In such circumstances, people who see themselves as "victims" of the wrongdoing or insensitivity of others will often be looking for someone to "rescue" them, and we need to keep our wits about us if we are not to be drawn into conflicts and ascribed a role we did not sign up for, or do not see as appropriate.

The drama triangle involves three "players".

▶ The victim

This person has a real or imagined understanding that someone is doing them harm, is bringing a threat to their happiness, or is in some way persecuting them.

▶ The persecutor

This person is perceived by the "victim" as the guilty party, as the person responsible for causing the problems.

▶ The rescuer

This is the person who is seen by the "victim" as an avenue for addressing the problems caused by the "persecutor".

The problem with this triangle is that it involves the development of an unhealthy dynamic. Members of the helping professions can be a prime target for being seen as a "rescuer" – seduced into taking sides and losing neutrality, perhaps only to find out later that the victim's perception of being persecuted was not an accurate one (it is sometimes the case that it turns out to be the "victim" who has been doing the persecuting). The drama triangle can lead us to adopt one person's partial interpretation instead of developing our own more holistic, thorough and impartial assessment. Being aware of the dangers of the drama triangle can help us to avoid falling into the trap of being drawn into taking sides.'

Thompson S and Thompson N (2018) *The Critically Reflective Practitioner* (2nd edition). London: Palgrave.

Worksheet 11: Avoiding the drama triangle

How might you recognise the drama triangle beginning to develop?

What sort of situations within your work setting might produce a drama triangle situation? Try to list at least three.

What strategies are available to you to prevent the drama triangle from developing?

What problems could arise from the drama triangle:

▶ for you as a supervisor?

▶ for supervisees involved?

▶ for the team or staff group as a whole?

Part Three: Conclusion

Conclusion

This manual has presented a wide range of resource materials, from the background materials in Part One through to the detailed training exercises laid out in Part Two. The role of Part Three is relatively straightforward – simply to draw together the main strands of the manual and to point you in the right direction for future learning.

This part of the manual will therefore:

▶ summarise the main themes that have emerged

▶ present ideas for further development through recommended reading, access to relevant organisations, websites and so on

▶ provide details of all the literature referred to in the text.

Supervision is an important part of human resource management, as it is a key way of helping to ensure that staff meet their full potential and gain maximum job satisfaction. High-quality reflective supervision is therefore potentially a major benefit for all concerned – staff, managers and the organisation as a whole. The time and effort it takes to develop a positive culture of supervision is therefore a small price to pay for the benefits that are to be had.

Supervision can be seen to comprise four main elements:

▶ *Accountability:* Supervisors share with their staff a responsibility to ensure that:

　▶ the necessary work tasks are undertaken

　▶ quality standards are as high as possible

　▶ relevant policies are adhered to

　▶ ethical standards are upheld.

▶ *Staff care:* Supporting staff is an important part of making sure that they are appropriately equipped to undertake their duties. Ensuring that staff are valued, supported and safe is therefore an important part of the supervisor's duties.

▶ *Staff development:* If continuous professional development is to become more than an empty slogan, then supervisors need to take seriously their duties in helping their staff learn and develop.

▶ *Mediation:* Supervisors are 'cogs' in the machinery that makes up an organisation. Part of the task is therefore to mediate between the interests and needs of particular staff and those of the organisation as a whole.

The main challenge that supervisors face is how to balance these four elements – that is, to ensure that all four are given adequate attention, rather than allowing one or more to predominate at the expense of the others.

The point was made earlier that supervision is concerned with 'the minimum and the maximum' – that is, on the one hand ensuring that acceptable standards are met, and on the other seeking to maximise potential with a view to achieving optimal outcomes for the benefit of everyone concerned. This is a far cry from the bureaucratic 'checking up' process that supervision has become for many people (if the comments of participants on courses we have run are anything to go by). We hope that the overview of key issues we have provided, together with the range of exercises presented, will provide a helpful platform for making sure that the positive potential of reflective supervision is realised and that, in tandem with the development of leadership skills, it is allowed to act as a basis for making working life as positive and effective an experience as it can be. We wish you well in your efforts to make reflective supervision an important contribution to personal and organisational effectiveness.

Guide to further learning

Recommended reading

Books

Human resource development/organisational learning

Beevers K and Rea A (2016) *Learning and Development Practice in the Workplace* (3rd edition). London: CIPD.

Carbery R and Cross C (Eds) (2015) *Human Resource Development: A Concise Introduction*. London: Palgrave.

Edgell S (2012) *The Sociology of Work: Continuity and Change in Paid and Unpaid Work* (2nd edition). London: Sage.

Honey P (2003) *101 Ways to Develop your People Without Really Trying: A Manager's Guide to Work Based Learning* (2nd edition). Maidenhead: Peter Honey Publications.

Linstead S, Fulop L and Lilley S (Eds) (2009) *Management and Organization: A Critical Text* (2nd edition). Basingstoke: Palgrave Macmillan.

McGuire D (2014) *Human Resource Development* (2nd edition). London: Sage.

Morgan G (2006) *Images of Organization* (3rd edition). London: Sage.

Rao A (2015) *Gender at Work: Theory and Practice for 21st Century Organizations*. London: Routledge.

Rees G and Smith PE (Eds) (2017) *Strategic Human Resource Management: An International Perspective* (2nd edition). London: Sage.

SCIE (2005) *Learning Organizations: A Self-assessment Resource Pack*. London: Social Care Institute for Excellence.

Senge PM (2006) *The Fifth Discipline: The Art and Practice of the Learning Organization*. London: Random House.

Taylor G Mellor L and McCarter R (2016) *Work-related Learning and the Social Sciences*. London: Routledge.

Thompson N (2013) *People Management*. Basingstoke: Palgrave Macmillan.

Thompson N (2018) *Promoting Equality: Working with Diversity and Difference* (4th edition). London: Palgrave.

Thompson N (2019) *The Learning from Practice Manual*. Wrexham: Avenue Media Solutions.

Thompson S and Thompson N (2018) *The Critically Reflective Practitioner* (2nd edition). London: Palgrave.

Watson TJ (2008) *Sociology, Work and Industry* (5th edition). London: Routledge.

Wilson FM (2003) *Organizational Behaviour and Gender* (2nd edition). Aldershot: Ashgate.

Wilson JP (Ed) (2005) *Human Resource Development: Learning and Training for Individuals and Organizations* (2nd edition). London: Kogan Page.

Supervision/Managing people

Doel M (2010) *Social Work Placements: A Traveller's Guide*. London: Routledge.

Doel M (2005) *New Approaches in Practice Learning*. London: Skills for Care.

Doel M, Sawdon C and Morrison D (2002) *Learning, Teaching and Assessment: Signposting the Portfolio*. London: Jessica Kingsley.

Doel M and Shardlow SM (2005) *Modern Social Work Practice: Teaching and Learning in Practice Settings*. Aldershot: Ashgate.

Field P, Jasper C and Littler L (2016) *Practice Education in Social Work: Achieving Professional Standards* (2nd edition). Northwich: Critical Publishing.

Lishman J (2015) *Handbook for Practice Learning in Social Work and Social Care: Knowledge and Theory* (3rd edition). London: Jessica Kingsley.

Morrison T (2006) *Supervision in Social Care* (3rd edition). Brighton: Pavilion.

Parker J (2010) *Effective Practice Learning in Social Work* (2nd edition). London: Sage.

Showell NW (2015) *Practice Educating Social Work Students: Supporting Students on Their Placements*. Maidenhead: Open University Press.

Coaching and mentoring

Clutterbuck D (1998) *Learning Alliances: Tapping into Talent*. London: Chartered Institute of Personnel and Development.

Clutterbuck D (2014) *Everyone Needs a Mentor* (5th edition). London: Kogan Page.

Clutterbuck D and Megginson D (2017) *Making Coaching Work*. London: Chartered Institute of Personnel and Development.

Gray DE, Garvey B and Lane DA (2016) *A Critical Introduction to Coaching and Mentoring*. London: Sage.

Parsloe E and Leedham M (2017) *Coaching and Mentoring: Practical Techniques for Developing Learning and Performance*. London: Kogan Page.

Starr J (2016) *The Coaching Manual: The Definitive Guide to the Process, Principles and Skills of Personal Coaching* (4th edition). Harlow: Pearson Education.

Other useful texts

Crawley J and Graham K (2002) *Mediation for Managers*. London: Nicholas Brealey.

De Bono E (1990) *Atlas of Management Thinking*. Harmondsworth: Penguin.

Doherty N and Guyler M (2008) *The Essential Guide to Workplace Mediation and Conflict Management*. London: Kogan Page.

Thompson N (2012) *The People Solutions Sourcebook* (2nd edition). Basingstoke: Palgrave Macmillan.

Thompson N (2015) *People Skills* (4th edition). London: Palgrave.

Training resources

Training manuals

Gilbert P and Thompson N (2019) *Developing Leadership: A Learning and Development Manual* (2nd edition). Brighton: Pavilion.

Morrison T (2006) *Staff Supervision in Social Care* (3rd edition). Brighton: Pavilion.

Thompson N (2019) *Promoting Equality, Valuing Diversity: A Learning and Development Manual* (2nd edition). Brighton: Pavilion Publishing.

Thompson N (2019) *Tackling Bullying and Harassment in the Workplace: A Learning and Development Manual* (2nd edition). Brighton: Pavilion.

Training DVDs

The following DVDs, presented by Neil Thompson, cover a range of issues very relevant to supervisors and managers:

Dealing with Stress, a three-DVD set: 'Understanding Stress'; 'Meeting the Stress Challenge' and 'Managing Stress'. Wrexham: Avenue Media Solutions.

Effective Leadership. Wrexham: Avenue Media Solutions.

Equality and Diversity: Neil Thompson on PCS Analysis. Wrexham: Avenue Media Solutions.

Managing Conflict. Wrexham: Avenue Media Solutions.

Reflective Practice. Wrexham: Avenue Media Solutions

E-learning courses

Neil Thompson has also been involved in developing a range of relevant e-learning courses:

Dealing with Stress

Developing a Reflective Practice Culture

Emotional Competence: Developing Emotional Intelligence and Resilience

Learning to Learn

Managing Equality, Diversity and Inclusion

Managing Stress (a follow-up course to Dealing with Stress specifically for managers)

Time and Workload Management

Organisations and websites

Here we provide details of a number of organisations that are concerned with various issues relating to supervision, staff development and related matters.

Campaign for Learning   www.campaign-for-learning.org.uk
19 Buckingham St
London WC2N 6EF
020 7798 6067

Chartered Institute of Personnel and Development   www.cipd.co.uk
151 The Broadway
London SW19 1JQ
020 8612 6208

Higher Education Academy   www.heacademy.ac.uk
Innovations Way
York Science Park
Heslington
York YO10 5BR
01904 717500

humansolutions   www.humansolutions.org.uk

A source of free information on workplace well-being issues, including barriers to learning.

National Learning and Work Institute

4th Floor, Arnhem House

31 Waterloo Way

Leicester LE1 6LP

01162 044200

References

Munro E (2011) *The Munro Review of Child Protection: Final Report. A Child-centred System.* London: The Stationery Office.

Roderick C (1993) *Becoming a learning organisation. Training and Development* **11** (3).

Rogers C (1961) *On Becoming a Person.* London: Constable.

Thompson N (2012) *The People Solutions Sourcebook.* Basingstoke: Palgrave Macmillan.

Thompson N (2013) *People Management.* Basingstoke: Palgrave Macmillan.

Thompson N (2018) *The Social Worker's Practice Manual.* Wrexham: Avenue Media Solutions.

Thompson N (2019a) *The Learning from Practice Manual.* Wrexham: Avenue Media Solutions.

Thompson N (2019b) *Promoting Equality, Valuing Diversity: A Learning and Development Manual* (2nd edition). Hove: Pavilion Publishing & Media.

Thompson N (2019c) *Tackling Bullying and Harassment in the Workplace: A Learning and Develpment Manual* (2nd edition). Hove: Pavilion Publishing & Media.

Thompson S and Thompson N (2018) *The Critically Reflective Practitioner* (2nd edition). London: Palgrave.

Appendix

Developing reflective supervision: a guide for new supervisors

This appendix has been provided so that you can photocopy it and use it as a handout on courses. It offers considerable helpful guidance that will help consolidate and reinforce whatever learning attendees gain from attending a course.

Developing reflective supervision: a guide for new supervisors

Supervision and leadership are two important facets of people management. Supervision involves working with staff on a one-to-one basis or in small groups, while leadership involves working more broadly with people, guiding them towards group goals and supporting them in doing so. Our focus here is on the important role of supervision in helping to ensure that staff are as fully equipped as possible to undertake their duties, in so far as: (i) they are clear about what is expected of them; (ii) they are enabled to learn from their experiences in order to keep abreast of developments and new demands; and (iii) they are adequately supported to ensure that the pressures of the work are manageable and not a source of harmful stress. In effect, supervision involves: keeping a clear focus on the goals we are trying to achieve; motivating staff to achieve optimal outcomes and maximise their own potential; contributing to a positive and constructive working environment; and seeking to ensure that staff's contributions are recognised and valued.

We shall approach the topic of supervision by seeing it in its broader context – that of human resource development.

What is human resource development?

Professional responsibility: more than a job

Acting as a supervisor involves not only making sure staff carry out their duties to at least a satisfactory standard, but also helping them to continue learning, developing and building on their existing strengths. Consequently, it can be helpful to think of your supervisory responsibilities under three headings:

Knowledge: In order to work effectively, there are certain things staff need to know. This will vary from job to job, but anything beyond the simplest of manual tasks involves some form of knowledge base.

Skills: Staff are expected to develop a range of skills, including interpersonal skills, stress management skills and practical skills. The expectation is not that staff should be experts, but they should be able to develop a range of skills to at least a basic standard of competence.

Values: Underpinning the work that you and your staff undertake will be a set of values – beliefs and assumptions which shape how you think and act. For example, in a retail setting, customer service is an important value to uphold. Without paying attention to such a value, it is unlikely that a retail business will thrive.

It is these three sets of factors that can make someone's work more than a job – elevating it to a vocation or profession that requires certain standards and brings with it certain rewards (see 'Job satisfaction' on p95). The question of professional responsibility is therefore an important one and not something that should be taken lightly. In view of this, staff development has to be seen as a vitally important issue, in so far as it has an essential role to play in terms of ensuring that staff are: aware of what their roles, tasks, duties and responsibilities are; well informed, well equipped and competent to do their job; kept up to date with developments in theory, practice, policy and law; motivated to do a good job and continue learning; confident but not complacent; learning from their mistakes and from their achievements; able to support each other; able to enjoy their work and gain job satisfaction; and motivated and equipped to take on new challenges.

Use of self

A commonly used term in the helping professions is 'use of self'. This refers to the fact that each individual has much to offer in terms of his or her own personality, experience, relationship skills and so on. Acting as a supervisor is a complex business that can test our personal resources: our resilience, patience, calmness, maturity, clear thinking and ability to work under pressure. All this involves use of self. In many occupations – particularly those that involve direct contact with people – use of self is also an important strength for staff to draw upon.

Consequently, the development of self through training and supervision is an important means of increasing effectiveness, reducing the number of mistakes made and increasing job satisfaction. Training and supervision can also play an important role in 'protecting' self – that is, human resources developments can help to improve stress management skills and help to ensure that staff are not harmed by the emotional pressures that come with many forms of work.

The significant role played by use of self means that staff development amounts to more than gaining basic knowledge and technical skills. If staff are to develop their potential to the full, there needs to be an understanding of the importance of use of self and opportunities for building on strengths and overcoming weaknesses. Professional development and personal development are closely intertwined.

Responsibility for learning

There are often many people involved in the process of learning: tutors, training officers, line managers, colleagues and so on. However, the most important person in all this is the individual learner – unless we take responsibility for our own learning, unless we are committed to developing our understanding and changing the way we think and act, learning will not take place.

Although others involved in the process can facilitate, support or encourage learning, they cannot make learning happen – it is only the individual who can do that ('You can lead a horse to water …'). Consequently, every member of staff has responsibility for his or her own learning.

For staff who have supervisory duties, the responsibility is twofold:

1. Being responsible for the supervision of others does not remove responsibility for one's own learning. No one, no matter how skilled or experienced they may be, ever reaches the point where they have nothing further to learn. Indeed, the attitude of 'I know everything I need to know' is a potentially very dangerous one.

2. Supervisory staff also have some degree of responsibility for facilitating and supporting the learning of the staff they supervise. This relates to both the specific examples of learning that arise in the process of supervision and the general duty to contribute to creating an atmosphere and working environment in which learning is welcomed, encouraged and rewarded.

Arguing that people are responsible for their own learning is not a means of 'passing the buck' – for example, by blaming poor quality training on the people who attended the course, rather than the person(s) who ran it. It is, however, a necessary acknowledgement of the fact that people will not learn unless they are committed to doing so, unless they take the necessary steps to make it happen. Human resource development, then, is not just a matter of providing training courses – it is a much broader matter that involves creating the right atmosphere for learning – relaxed and friendly, but not complacent or without challenge; supporting staff in their attempts to learn and develop their knowledge, skills and values; recognising, encouraging and using opportunities for learning; and dealing with mistakes constructively, rather than negatively.

It is also important to note that learning involves a process of change. If we are still the same after a learning experience, then what was the point of learning? Learning involves moving on, developing a new perspective and gaining new knowledge and/ or skills. Because of this process of change at the heart of learning, it can sometimes be painful and involve letting go of things which we have perhaps taken for granted for a very long time (a lot of learning about values and equality and diversity involves this type of 'letting go' or 'unlearning'). We should therefore be honest and acknowledge that learning can sometimes be difficult and demanding, reflecting the old saying: 'There's no gain without pain'.

Equality and diversity

In order to promote equality and affirm diversity, it is necessary to encourage approaches to work that are not based on prejudice or discrimination against particular individuals or groups; do not condone or reinforce existing inequalities – for example, by relying on stereotypes; challenge the discriminatory or oppressive actions and attitudes of others; and that recognise that we live in a 'diverse' society – that is, one where people come from many different backgrounds – and that we should not regard differences between people as problems or weaknesses.

We must therefore pay attention to basic questions of equality of opportunity in order to ensure that staff are able to develop their knowledge and skills in ways that are consistent with the value base. This includes the following: recognising the importance of each individual's cultural background or heritage and respecting his or her customs, practices, choice of food and so on; acknowledging the experience of disadvantage and oppression by certain groups and individuals as a result of racism, sexism, disablism and so on; and developing sensitivity to the ways in which stereotypes and unquestioned assumptions can reinforce inequality and disadvantage – for example, through assumptions that people with disabilities cannot make decisions for themselves.

Consequently, equality and the potential for discrimination need to be recurring themes within the human resource development process.

Lifelong learning

Reflective practice

One of the dangers associated with working life is the potential for developing 'routinised practice', a way of working characterised by unthinking routines where we are operating on 'automatic pilot'. This is a dangerous form of practice because:

▶ important aspects of a situation may not be recognised because the uniqueness of each set of circumstances may not be appreciated

▶ the wrong approach may be used – trying to fit a square peg into a round hole

▶ customers, service users or other important stakeholders may get the impression that their specific needs or circumstances are not being taken into consideration, that they are not valued or important

▶ it stifles creativity and the use of imaginative approaches

▶ it limits opportunities for gaining job satisfaction.

This is not to say that routines have no place in working life – clearly they do. A set of routines can be a significant source of a sense of security, a sense of 'rhythm' and familiarity. Routines are also important ways of saving time and energy by undertaking repetitive tasks in as efficient a way as possible. However, an important skill is that of being able to distinguish between when a routine is appropriate and harmless, and when such a routine would be inappropriate and therefore dangerous. That is, we have to recognise that many things cannot be safely dealt with as a matter of routine.

Job satisfaction

Working with people makes various demands upon us, but also brings many rewards. It is important to recognise that job satisfaction is like a form of fuel that keeps us going. Without it, there is a danger that we may get worn down, lacking in energy, motivation or commitment. And this can be the beginning of a vicious circle. If we don't get job satisfaction, if we don't get the necessary rewards and satisfactions from our work, we are less likely to be effective or to work with flair and imagination, because we are less highly motivated, less likely to be 'on top form'.

If we are not motivated and committed to what we are doing, we are much less likely to achieve any job satisfaction – a circle has been set up, a vicious circle in which two destructive aspects (low job satisfaction and low standards of practice) reinforce each other, thereby increasing the destructive potential of the situation. Consequently, job satisfaction has to be seen as a key issue in maintaining high standards of practice.

Human resource development has a part to play in maintaining and enhancing levels of job satisfaction. This applies in a number of ways:

▶ by encouraging staff to reflect on their practice and appreciate achievements gained, progress made and lessons learned

▶ by developing confidence and skills

▶ by providing a wider range of options to draw on

▶ by providing a sense of achievement, progress and direction.

Keeping up to date

Working life is not 'static' – situations change, new circumstances arise, new developments occur, things move on. For example, a new development in one's work brings a fresh set of challenges, a new set of issues to address. Consequently, staff have a duty to keep up to date with such developments. These include:

▶ new ideas that can improve practice

▶ changes in policy or procedures

▶ changes in the law or statutory guidance

▶ learning from new research or other developments in the knowledge base.

This does not mean that staff have to have their noses in books for long periods of time. It does, however, mean that – for many grades of staff, at least – there is an expectation that some effort is made to read about new developments, to share ideas and help keep one another up to date.

Keeping up to date with important developments should not be seen as a chore, but rather as a fairly normal activity as part of the overall process of staff development. In this way it becomes part of lifelong learning, as well as a further potential source of job satisfaction.

Investing in people

Cost or investment?

Staff are usually the most expensive resource in an organisation. That is, the costs of maintaining a workforce usually exceed any other costs the organisation has to bear. This is particularly the case in the helping professions, where people's skills, knowledge and commitment are so vitally important. However, there is a danger in seeing the situation mainly in terms of costs. A more helpful approach is to think of the money spent on staff as an investment, rather than simply a set of costs.

Human resource development involves a considerable investment of time, effort, energy and money. However, the benefits to be gained from an effective system of staff development can be seen to outweigh these costs. These benefits should not be underestimated, because they:

▶ are an important part of having a well-informed, confident and committed group of staff

▶ create a positive working environment in which staff feel valued and supported

▶ reduce the chances of costly mistakes being made

▶ enhance the reputation and standing of the organisation

▶ improve levels of service and the quality of life of customers, service users and so on.

It is therefore important to recognise that staff development is an essential investment in good practice rather than a drain on the organisation's resources.

Staff care

It has long been recognised that working life has the potential to be very stressful. It involves a number of pressures that can, if they are not dealt with appropriately, cause considerable harm. These pressures include:

▶ the physical demands of the various tasks associated with many jobs – not just manual jobs, but also a wide range of posts that can be physically demanding

▶ the risk of encountering aggression and violence in some situations – sadly not as uncommon an occurrence as we would like

▶ the emotional demands that arise as a result of the potential conflicts and tensions involved in various work settings – whether in public service or the commercial world

▶ the risk of getting things wrong and doing harm instead of good – something that can apply in any form of work.

Dealing with stress is partly an individual responsibility, but not entirely so. Organisations also have a degree of responsibility for ensuring that their staff are not exposed to excessive levels of stress. In some ways, this is a reflection of health and safety responsibilities, and is partly a question of good management practice in ensuring that there is an ethos of 'staff care' or 'workplace well-being'.

Staff care is a term that refers to the various steps that employers can or do take to promote the well-being of their staff, so that they are able to fulfil their duties effectively and gain satisfaction from doing so. These steps include induction, supervision, appraisal and grievance procedures; maternity and paternity leave; and, of course, training and staff development. Human resource development is a key element in the overall process of staff care, and staff care, in turn, is an important part of investing in people.

Healthy organisations

Some organisations work in such a way that they have a very detrimental effect on their staff. Work is an important part of people's lives, and so problems or tensions at work can have a very significant effect on our health and well-being. No organisation will be perfect or ideally suited to staff, of course, but some are certainly much better than others when it comes to providing a positive environment in which to work.

One of the things that can be associated with organisations that cause undue problems for their staff is a failure to support staff in developing the knowledge, skills and values necessary to carry out the work successfully and satisfyingly. A healthy organisation is therefore one that, among other things, provides the necessary backing for staff to carry out their duties effectively and gain job satisfaction from doing so.

A key part of this backing that an organisation must provide is an appropriate system of human resource development, one which continuously provides opportunities for learning, encourages learning, discourages defensiveness and allows people to be open about their learning needs without fear of undue criticism, and continues to make staff development a priority, even though this may be difficult at times due to other pressures.

Making supervision work

What is supervision?

Literally, the term 'supervision' refers to the process of 'watching over'. However, we should not see it too literally as a process of 'keeping an eye on' staff. The reality of supervision is far more complex than that.

Supervision is basically the process organisations use to manage the relationship between the overall organisation and its needs on the one hand, and the individual and his or her needs on the other. Sometimes the two sets of needs are compatible, but at other times there may be a degree of conflict or tension.

The supervisor's task can therefore be seen as: (i) helping to make the most of those aspects of working life where the individual and the organisation are 'on the same wavelength' and a lot of progress can be achieved (for example, where the organisation's need for high-quality practice overlaps with the individual staff member's need for job satisfaction); (ii) managing the tension between the organisation and the individual where there isn't such an overlap (for example, where a new policy may be resisted because one or more members of staff disapprove of it or an aspect of it).

The specific tasks involved and their importance should become clearer in the pages that follow.

Who am I responsible for?

This question affirms that it is vitally important that you are aware of which particular members of staff you are responsible for in terms of their development. This is a particularly important responsibility, in so far as it involves sharing responsibility for other people's work in terms of standards of practice (accountability), support (staff care) and learning (continuous professional development). These are discussed in more detail below. The bottom line, however, is that, if something goes wrong for one of the staff you supervise, you may share some degree of responsibility for the situation.

In view of the fact that your supervisory responsibilities are so important, it is essential that you are completely clear about which members of staff you are responsible for. If you supervise staff who are themselves supervisors (either of other staff or of students on placement), don't forget you will need to ensure that they too are taking their supervisory responsibilities seriously.

Of course, another important factor to consider is: who is responsible for supervising you? Clear expectations about the nature of supervisory relationships and their implications are an important part of a healthy organisation. However, this is a two-way process. If the system is to work smoothly and to maximum effect, it is important that supervisors and supervisees work co-operatively together. You therefore need to consider not one set of issues but two:

1. How can I make sure that my supervision of staff is as good as it possibly can be?

2. How can I make the best possible use of the supervision I receive?

What are my responsibilities?

Supervisory responsibilities can be divided into four categories: accountability, staff care, staff development and mediation.

Accountability: Organisations usually work on the basis that supervisors are accountable for the actions of their staff. That is, where basic-grade staff act in a particular way, the supervisor concerned shares some degree of responsibility for those actions – this is the basis of accountability. Consequently, it is very important that supervisors recognise their responsibilities for others. If this doesn't happen, there is a very real danger that the errors of staff will backfire on their supervisors. And, ironically, if supervisory staff are not taking their accountability role seriously, the likelihood of mistakes being made is that much higher, as opportunities to 'nip them in the bud' will be missed.

Staff care: The importance of staff care has already been emphasised. Supervisory staff have a very important role to play in terms of making sure that staff feel valued and adequately supported. A supportive line manager is a major benefit for a staff member, whereas an unsupportive one can be a source of resentment and ill feeling. Staff care plays an important role in helping staff fend off stress and its harmful effects on health, relationships, standard of work and so on.

Staff development: A common misunderstanding of supervision is that it is primarily, if not exclusively, about accountability. The responsibility for helping staff learn and develop is one that is often neglected in many organisations. This is partly because many supervisors feel uncomfortable with the role. They are much happier with a managerial accountability role and don't feel very happy addressing people's learning needs or helping to remove barriers to learning. However, promoting learning is a crucial part of the work of anyone with supervisory responsibilities.

Mediation: Sometimes it is necessary to act as a 'mediator' between one or more of the staff that you supervise and other parts of the organisation. For example, a member of staff may have a grievance against the organisation and may need your support to get the matter resolved. This role is sometimes referred to as 'fighting up, selling down' – that is, representing the interests of staff (fighting up) has to be balanced against representing the organisation (selling down or 'cooling out'). Handling this tension (and keeping both sides happy) is a highly skilled job and needs to be taken very seriously. If you neglect the staff you supervise, they will resent you and will not trust you, thereby making your job very difficult. If, on the other hand, you act against the interests of the organisation, you could again be making your job a lot harder by creating conflict between yourself and your employers – and this too could backfire on your staff.

Why should I bother?

There are various reasons why you should not adopt a 'Why bother?' attitude, not least of which is the fact that you would not be doing your job properly! However, one reason that is particularly important is what can be called the 'doubling' effect. Look at it this way: if you play an active part in developing your staff, you will be contributing positively to standards of practice, levels of skill and knowledge, motivation, job satisfaction and so on. However, where development issues are neglected or discouraged, the net result can be one of resentment, ill feeling and mistrust – all of which can undermine confidence, motivation and quality of work. The difference between the two is therefore double.

Troubleshooting

Resistance and non-cooperation

Sometimes staff members do not understand or appreciate the nature or importance of continuous professional development. Similarly, some people may feel threatened by development issues – they may see it as something that may reveal their weaknesses or undermine their confidence (this can apply in relation to both training courses and supervision). For others, it may simply be a question of the fear of the unknown. But, whatever the reasons, the outcome is likely to be resistance and/or a lack of co-operation – in other words, serious obstacles to learning. Consequently, it is important that strategies are developed to counteract such resistance sensitively and constructively. These can include:

▶ *talking things through* – often anxieties, misconceptions and other barriers to learning can be removed by talking them through, either in supervision or more informally

▶ *naming the process* – where someone is displaying resistance, for example by changing the subject whenever certain issues are raised, it can be very effective to name the process, to state explicitly what is happening ('There you go again, you're changing the subject')

▶ *sticking with it* – it is not uncommon for people to show some degree of resistance initially, but then to begin to warm to the idea and settle down. It's therefore important not to overreact and start tackling the issues too soon. They will often sort themselves out fairly quickly.

Personality clashes

There may well be times when the supervisor and a staff member do not see eye to eye, when personality differences get in the way of good working relations. This can cause serious difficulties in terms of a positive atmosphere for learning. A personality clash can cause great tensions – tensions that prevent positive learning. Consequently, there is a need for staff with supervisory responsibilities to take steps to ensure that personality clashes are avoided or their effects minimised. These include:

▶ *Assertiveness:* Finding a helpful balance between being submissive and being domineering can help to keep conflicts to a minimum, or avoid them altogether.

▶ *Unconditional positive regard:* This is an idea put forward by Carl Rogers (1961). It means that we should adopt a positive attitude towards the people we are trying to help, regardless of who they are or what they may have done. In this context, it would involve putting any personal feelings to one side and maintaining a positive professional working relationship.

▶ *Clearing the air:* Sometimes the tensions between people can become so great that it is necessary to 'clear the air' – to address the situation directly. This does not have to involve being confrontational, but it does mean being prepared to discuss differences openly, honestly and constructively.

▶ *Third party support:* At times it may become necessary to involve a third person to help resolve difficulties, acting as a 'mediator'. This is a relatively rare occurrence but, if used sensitively, can be a turning point in a difficult relationship or situation.

NB Although personality clashes can cause a lot of problems, it should be remembered that the relationship between staff is, ultimately, a professional one geared towards providing high standards of practice. It is therefore the responsibility of all staff, but supervisory staff in particular, to take all reasonable steps to prevent personal differences from getting in the way of effective practice.

Workload management

The old saying 'you can't fit a quart into a pint pot' has a lot of truth in it. That is, there is only so much work that an individual can do in a given day. Consequently, it is understandable that staff may sometimes claim that they are too busy to get involved in staff development activities or that they are too busy to take the time to reflect on their work and learn from it. However, although it is understandable, it is still a problem that needs to be addressed and resolved. It is therefore very important to take seriously the question of workload management.

In view of the importance of staff development in terms of motivation, job satisfaction and standards of work, it really is a false economy to neglect staff development because we are 'too busy'. This is parallelled with the driver who is too busy to have his or her car serviced or maintained and then finds that a great deal of time is wasted when it breaks down.

Staff can be helped, encouraged and supported in managing their workload effectively so that staff development does not get pushed to one side by other pressures. This can be done in a variety of ways:

▶ *Setting priorities* – 'First things first' is an important motto. When people are busy or under pressure it is relatively easy to lose track of priorities. When this happens there is a danger that very important things are not done while less important matters receive attention. A clear focus on priorities is therefore an important part of staff development.

▶ *Maintaining motivation* – managing a workload is not just a question of managing time; it also involves managing levels of energy and motivation. If staff are keen and motivated they will achieve a lot more than if they are feeling bored, unstimulated or generally lacking in motivation. This brings us back to the key issue of job satisfaction discussed above.

▶ *Reviewing work regularly* – an important part of workload management is having a sense of control. A sense of control reduces anxiety and increases confidence, motivation and clarity of purpose. Regular reviews of work tasks (to measure progress and identify what remains to be done) can play a very important part in developing and maintaining that sense of control.

What about my staff development?

Responsibility for learning

The point was emphasised earlier that learning is primarily the task of the learner. This applies not only when supporting other people in their learning, but also in managing and developing our own learning. We therefore have to be clear about what steps we are taking to ensure that we too are learning. It is very easy for people who are concerned with the learning of others to neglect their own learning – to get wrapped up in helping others without helping themselves. Being responsible for supporting the learning and development of others does not take away our responsibility for our own learning.

The learning organisation

The notion of the 'learning organisation' is a very important one. A learning organisation, as the name implies, makes learning a priority. Roderick (1993) explains that learning organisations:

▶ *'take every opportunity to learn both from experience and in general at individual, group and corporate level;*

▶ *experiment with new ways of organising work and new ways of learning both within and outside the organisation;*

▶ *establish a climate in which learning from each other is actively supported;*

▶ *use the training function to facilitate the development and learning of all employees; see a key role for managers as facilitators;*

▶ *develop structures which encourage two-way communication as a means of promoting learning and development;*

▶ *encourage questioning, experimentation and exploration of new ideas at all levels; remove barriers and blockages to learning in both the individual and the environment;*

▶ *encourage and foster continuous learning and self-development in all employees; think about how to learn as well as what to learn.'*

(p13)

All employees, especially those with supervisory responsibilities, have an important part to play in building and maintaining a learning organisation. In pursuing your own staff development as well as supporting others, you are contributing to the development of a learning organisation.

Part of the solution or part of the problem?

In making a positive contribution to staff development, we take steps towards achieving positive outcomes and increased levels of job satisfaction. If, however, we do not make such a positive contribution, we may be undermining quality of work and job satisfaction. This is because, in neglecting our staff development role, we are contributing to the problem rather than the solution – we are giving the impression that unthinking, uncritical practice is acceptable, that it is not necessary for staff to learn and develop. There is a responsibility for supervisory staff to 'set a good example' by taking very seriously their own learning needs and doing something positive about them. We cannot expect staff to demonstrate a commitment to staff development and lifelong learning if their supervisors do not do the same.

Conclusion

Commitment to staff development can be a major strength of any organisation. In order to make the most of that strength, we feel very strongly that staff development must be undertaken in partnership. It requires a commitment from all concerned if high standards are to be achieved and maintained. This involves contributing the time, effort, energy and vision required for:

▶ *supervisors* – to support staff in their learning and to ensure that supervision is more than a tokenistic attempt to appear supportive

▶ *all staff* – to play an active role in continuing to learn and develop, continuously enhancing standards of practice and levels of job satisfaction

▶ *senior managers* – to fund and manage staff development and make any changes that become necessary in order to maximise its effectiveness.

This sounds like a major organisational commitment – and indeed it is – but it offers immense benefits in a number of ways. A lack of commitment to staff development, by contrast, is a false economy that has many costs for staff, for the organisation as a whole, but most of all for the people the organisation serves.

Reflective supervision involves not only creating a reflective space for personal and professional development within supervision itself, but also helping staff to develop and sustain reflective approaches to their practice in general. Achieving success in this regard involves recognising that supervision must be much more than a process of case or task management (which can disempower the worker and prevent the development of their decision-making skills and their confidence). It must incorporate all four elements (accountability, staff development, staff care and mediation); it must be geared towards achieving the *maximum* (helping the supervisee to be the best possible worker they can be), and not just the *minimum* of making sure that they are doing their job properly. It must also be a two-way professional process, with the supervisee fully and actively engaged in the process, and not a one-way bureaucratic process where instructions are issued or all that happens is a process of 'checking up' ('snoopervision').

If that makes being a supervisor sound quite demanding, that is because it is. However, the rewards for all concerned far outweigh the efforts needed to make effective reflective supervision a reality.

Dr Neil Thompson

Neil is an independent writer, educator and adviser. He is the author of *The Learning from Practice Manual* (Avenue Media Solutions, 2019), the producer of a range of e-learning courses and the director of an innovative online learning community, the Avenue Professional Development Programme, based on principles of self-directed learning and geared towards developing reflective practice. His website is at www.NeilThompson.info.